OUT THERE ADIRONDACKS

108 OF THE WEIRDEST, WILDEST, AND MOST WONDERFUL ATTRACTIONS OF THE ADIRONDACK REGION

LARRY WEILL

BOOKS
NORTH COUNTRY BOOKS

North Country Books
An imprint of The Globe Pequot Publishing Group, Inc.
64 South Main Street
Essex, CT 06426
www.globepequot.com

Distributed by NATIONAL BOOK NETWORK

British Library Cataloguing in Publication Information available

Library of Congress Cataloging-in-Publication Data

Names: Weill, Larry, author.
Title: Out there Adirondacks : 108 of the weirdest, wildest, and most
  wonderful attractions of the Adirondack Region / Larry Weill.
Other titles: 108 of the weirdest, wildest, and most wonderful attractions
  of the Adirondack Region
Description: Lanham, MD : North Country Books, [2024] | Summary: "Bursting
  with photos and insider tips, this fun and fascinating guide to the
  Adirondacks showcases more than 100 obscure and off-the-beaten-path sites in
  and around The Blue Line"—Provided by publisher.
Identifiers: LCCN 2024016053 (print) | LCCN 2024016054 (ebook) | ISBN
  9781493078929 (paperback) | ISBN 9781493078936 (epub)
Subjects: LCSH: Adirondack Mountains Region (N.Y.)—Guidebooks. | Historic
  Sites—New York (State)—Adirondack Mountains Region—Guidebooks. |
  Curiosities and wonders—New York (State)—Adirondack Mountains
  Region—Guidebooks. | Adirondack Mountains Region (N.Y.)—History,
  Local. | Adirondack Park (N.Y.)—Guidebooks.
Classification: LCC F127.A2 W386 2025 (print) | LCC F127.A2 (ebook) | DDC
  917.47/504—dc23/eng/20240705
LC record available at https://lccn.loc.gov/2024016053
LC ebook record available at https://lccn.loc.gov/2024016054

∞™ The paper used in this publication meets the minimum requirements of American National Standard for Information Sciences—Permanence of Paper for Printed Library Materials, ANSI/NISO Z39.48-1992.

CONTENTS

Preface   v

Attractions of Warren County   1

Attractions of Hamilton County   49

Attractions of Franklin County   83

Attractions of Fulton County   115

Attractions of Lewis County   135

Attractions of Jefferson County   147

Attractions of Essex County   155

Attractions of Oneida County   171

Attractions of Washington County   177

Attractions of Herkimer County   187

Attractions of Saratoga County   197

Attractions of St. Lawrence County   205

Attractions of Clinton County   209

Acknowledgments   217

PREFACE

The Adirondack Park is a huge and diverse region that has earned its place in the hearts of millions. From those who live within the confines of New York State to those who reside elsewhere, the park hosts throngs of visitors every year who come to enjoy its natural and man-made attractions. Many of these visitors return each year to the same destination, whether that be a particular town, a camp, or even a favorite swimming hole. The trip becomes a family tradition that is often handed down from one generation to the next.

As such, many visitors to the Adirondacks tend to get "zoomed in" on a single geographic location. They may become experts in all that surrounds the Great Sacandaga Lake, or Raquette Lake, or Lake Placid and the High Peaks, without ever venturing out into the rest of the 6.3 million acres of land known as the Adirondack Park. This is a shame given the multitude of attractions spread across the territory, many of which are known only to local residents.

When I set out to prepare this book, I wanted it to be different from the vast array of current Adirondack guides. Books that document the lakes and trails of the region, along with those that present the major attractions known as "tourist traps," already exist. Many of these attractions, such as Ausable Chasm, have been open for over a hundred years. (Ausable Chasm has been open to the public since 1870.) But this text looks in a different direction: to the unusual, the bizarre, the historic, and the sometimes unknown.

In these pages, you will read about the lesser-known sites inside "The Blue Line," including sights such as "George," the monster of Lake George, as well as the world's largest glove, ghosts swimming in Nine Corner Lake, and the annual Sasquatch-Calling Festival. You will see where some of the most famous characters in Adirondack history are buried and find out about the history of the only woman ever hanged in the state of New York. You will also learn of numerous sites and events that are not well-known to the public, including a vacant Cold War–era nuclear missile silo outside Saranac Lake and a Sasquatch-Calling Festival in Whitehall. Many of these sights are linked directly to the history of the Adirondack Park, while others are presented purely for their frivolous or unusual aspects. Either way, most either have been overlooked or are completely unknown to the average visitor to the park.

I have tried to arrange these attractions on a county-by-county basis. Each is located in a county that is at least partially situated inside the park, although some counties (e.g., Lewis County) have only a slim portion of their territories inside the Blue Line. Whenever possible, I have attempted to concentrate on attractions that are actually inside the park itself. However, there are a great many sites located in "Adirondack counties" (partially contained inside the Blue Line) that are situated outside the park. I've included these as "honorable mention" attractions that were just too good to pass up. On at least one occasion, the location of the attraction was literally a few hundred feet from the "Entering Adirondack Park" sign.

I also must admit some of these attractions were chosen at random, since to list and describe every extraordinary location would be impossible. For example, there are just too many ghost towns scattered throughout the park to include all of them in this text. The gentleman who guided me to the remnants of Wardboro recalled that there were probably twenty such locations just in his county. Some of these localities are more intact than others, although the state of decay actually contributes to the "eeriness" of the setting. It certainly tweaks the imagination to be walking through the tall grass and weeds in the middle of a deep forest and suddenly come upon row after row of ancient gravestones. Their stories just beg to be told, but all too often there are no surviving residents of the original settlements left to recount the memories.

Most (but not all) of these attractions are free to the public, including almost all of the historic sights and public buildings. There are a few, mainly related to the conventions and competitions, that do charge a fee, as do some of the museums.

It is also important to point out that not all of these attractions are "open to the public." Some of them, while easily observed from the side of the road, are located on private property and do not welcome visitors unless previously invited. We request that you respect the privacy of these individuals and admire their attractions without intruding on their grounds.

Finally, I'd like to say that writing this book was one of the more pleasant and rewarding experiences of my literary career. It wasn't so much the activity involved in finding and exploring many of these sights as the people with whom I worked in the process. They varied in their roles, from county and town historians to guides to common folks I encountered in my perambulations throughout the park. Some of these individuals had more defined roles and were responsible for knowing the sights within their territories. In some cases, these folks either created works of art that are in the view of the public or owned a residence or other structure of historic interest, and they were outwardly friendly in sharing their knowledge and stories with me. However, others were merely chance encounters who learned of my quest through overheard conversations, then stepped in to lead me to some hitherto unknown (to me) attraction. But regardless of who they were and what their assigned roles were, they were all incredibly helpful and friendly. Working with all these wonderful people who were willing to share their time and knowledge was truly an amazing experience that I found utterly heartwarming.

So feel free to explore as few or as many of these strange and unusual locations as you desire. Either way, you will have some great stories to tell when you return home at the end of your vacation. But please, try to avoid being devoured by the Sasquatch or attacked by the Lake George Monster. It's much more fun to read about their history than to become part of it.

ATTRACTIONS OF WARREN COUNTY

LAKE GEORGE "MYSTERY SPOT"

Hello hello hello hello. No, this isn't a misprint. But you will be hearing yourself speak over and over again if you stop by this mysterious, circular brick structure on an unmarked platform in the middle of Lake George known as the Lake George "Mystery Spot." Located off Beach Road near the Lake George Visitor Center, it hardly stands out from its surroundings. Yet its audio features have

View of Lake George over the Lake George "Mystery Spot" in downtown Lake George.

made it popular with visitors, who stop by to hear their voices echo softly around the circular structure.

Whether this site was designed to have such an unusual effect on sound is debatable. You will find no signs posted saying "Stand here" or "Listen to this." You just have to know where you are and then stand in the middle of the circle. (It is easy to find the center, due to the pattern of lines and circles on the base.)

Once situated at the epicenter, face the lakefront and say something, preferably directing your voice straight out rather than looking up. The effect is rather eerie and can vary from a "murmuring" undertone to a full-scale echo. The reverberation is caused by the bounce-back effect of the sound waves from the surrounding circular bricks. Structures such as this have been constructed intentionally, often as part of museum displays and such, but this appears to be a complete accident. Benches for seating are situated around the inside of the circle, and it is rather amusing to see the expressions of visitors taking a rest break as you stand alone in the circle and start talking aloud. (Especially if they are unaware of the unusual acoustic phenomenon.) But that just adds to the attraction.

This is not a site that warrants a lengthy side trip to visit, but it is interesting if you are already in the area.

IT'S A MONSTER, BY GEORGE!

Want to increase tourism while simultaneously having a little fun? Why not create your very own lake monster and see where it leads? This was the idea of Mr. Harry Waltrous, a painter and visitor to Lake George in 1904.

"Georgie" in his display case in the front foyer of the town of Hague Community Center.

PHOTO BY LARRY WEILL

This story traces its roots to a competitive friendship in the early days of the twentieth century. The two friends, Harry Waltrous and William Mann, were both avid fishermen who fought to land the biggest fish between them. Mann used some deception to supposedly catch and then display a whopper lake trout that weighed in at more than 40 pounds. However, the fish wasn't real; Waltrous determined that it was actually a wooden recreation.

Not to be outdone, Waltrous resorted to some playful

The Lake George monster emerging from the depths of Lake George, on display at the town of Hague Community Center.
PHOTO BY LARRY WEILL

duplicity of his own and created a veritable monster from a 10-foot-long cedar log. Using a pair of large green glass insulators to fashion the bulging eyes and red paint around its venomous-looking teeth, he produced a serpent of massive proportions. He then contrived a rope-and-pulley system to maneuver the monster up from the depths of the lake, where it surfaced and greeted boaters from the local hotels. According to some accounts, "Georgie" caused more than one boat to capsize and was even responsible for the divorce of a young couple when the husband fled the water for shore without rescuing his young bride from the ensuing debacle.

Due to numerous factors, Georgie eventually fell into disuse and was moved several times as ownership was transferred, ending up as far away as St. Thomas in the US Virgin Islands. He was eventually returned to the United States, where he now resides in the Lake George Historical Association at 290 Canada Street in Lake George. Visit the Lake George Historical Association website for hours of operation (www.lakegeorgehistorical.org). A smaller duplicate can also be viewed, along with all the interesting stories, at the town of Hague Community Center at 9793 Graphite Mountain Road, Hague, New York. Contact https://townofhague.org for hours of operation.

MARILYN MONROE'S DREAM HOUSE (WARRENSBURG)

What's more exciting than winning a house as a contest prize? How about getting the keys to the prize dwelling handed to you by none other than rising blond bombshell actress Marilyn Monroe. (Her legal name was still Norma Jeane Mortenson.) That alone would have made this event extremely popular, even in 1949.

This story was never widely publicized outside of the local area, and it has largely faded from memory with the passing of time. But, in 1949, the young and not-yet-famous starlet named Marilyn was chosen by *Photoplay Magazine* to be the designated presenter of its contest's grand prize. At the time, Monroe was publicizing her new film, *Love Happy*, and the contest was meant to create interest in the actress's budding career on the silver screen. The winner was a widow, Virginia McAllister, who would have been even more thrilled had she known of the future fame of Marilyn Monroe. (Monroe was only 22 years old at the time of the contest.)

The prefabricated house was not large by today's standards. In fact, it had just two bedrooms, a small kitchen, a living room, and little else. However, in 1949, there was still a postwar housing shortage, which resulted in the magazine receiving some 250,000 entries. So even the thought of being handed the deed to a house that was completely paid in full was a major story indeed.

That house still stands on the lot at 13 James Street, witness to the passage of 75 years of time. The property is owned by Ms. Polly Arehart, who also owns and lives in the house next door. Arehart has seen the house pass from one owner to another during her time in Warrensburg and is sentimental about the residence that is still connected to Marilyn Monroe.

"It's a nice little place, and it's got such an unusual history attached to it," Arehart said. "In a way, I'm sort of considering moving into it myself, since my own house is way too big for me. So I might just move in and see if I can find the ghost of Norma Jeane in there somewhere."

The house looks much like it did in 1949, with the exception of a wheelchair ramp that accesses the front entry. Much of its frontage is shrouded by some large, overgrown shrubs that serve to camouflage the building from the street. But very little could hide the history of this house from the public, most of whom would drive by without ever giving it a second glance.

ELEPHANTS ON THE LOOSE IN THE ADIRONDACKS

The Adirondack Park is full of animals of all kinds, including beaver, deer, black bear, and even the occasional moose. But elephants? Seriously?

This artistic rendering was the work of local Hague resident Michael Coffin, who sometime around 1980 noticed that a large, gray rock formation along the side of NY Route 8 resembled the head and trunk of an elephant. Coffin then

Elephant Rock on NY Route 8 outside Hague.

Photo by Larry Weill

went to work with a bucket of paint and a boatload of imagination and added a pair of eyes and a curved set of tusks, thus bringing the creature to life. The rock formation is painted on both sides, thus making the elephant visible when approaching from either direction.

The playful pachyderm has endured ever since and is a favorite landmark of vacationers passing by en route to points west. Similar to Pig Rock (located near Speculator, New York), this monolith also survived an attempt by the state highway department to blast it to pieces during a highway improvement project. The local residents banded together, and the public uproar led to the project being altered to preserve the entirety of the beast.

Elephant Rock can be found 3–4 miles west of the town of Hague on Route 8, on the south side of the highway. Viewers are warned, however, that extreme caution must be taken when stopping to see it, as the rock is situated on a sharp curve in the road, which can be dangerous due to passing traffic.

GHOSTS ABOUT THE SAGAMORE

The Sagamore Hotel, located in the town of Bolton Landing, is situated on a small private island (Green Island) on Lake George. It originally opened its doors to Adirondack travelers in 1883 and since that time has enjoyed a reputation for providing luxury accommodations to wealthy clientele.

The Sagamore also has a long record of stories and fables to accompany its lengthy history. The hotel was twice damaged by fire but was rebuilt to even higher levels of opulence in 1921, when it resumed its high-end reputation for serving the affluent tourists of the day. The hotel was closed for a couple of years in the 1980s when it fell on hard times, but it was permanently restored and reopened in 1983 in its formerly majestic configuration.

Front entrance of the stately Sagamore Hotel in Bolton Landing.
PHOTO BY LARRY WEILL

Of greater interest to many guests than the historic background is the record of ghostly sightings and other paranormal activity. The hotel, which is listed in the National Register of Historic Places, also appears on *Today Magazine*'s list of "Top 10 Most Haunted Hotels in the US." Stories abound of ghosts, both male and female, who float about the rooms and hallways of the stately facility, sometimes electing to be seen, while at other times remaining invisible.

Bar room inside the Sagamore, where several hotel bartenders have experienced "unusual phenomena" and sightings.
PHOTO BY LARRY WEILL

One of the front desk attendants told an interesting personal story. He was performing a late-night check of some business meeting rooms on the lower floor. When he was walking past one of the large meeting/event rooms, which was closed for the night, the doors suddenly opened as if inviting him in. (The room did not have automatic doors.) As the employee leaned forward to look for the cause of the doors opening, the lights in the room suddenly came on.

In another story told by a staff member, a female employee was making her way down one of the upper floor hallways when she felt her arm being pulled backward, as if by an unseen hand. She turned quickly and saw the material on her long sleeve being pulled, as if held in an invisible grip. Rather than investigate the paranormal experience, the frightened employee ran to a nearby office, where she locked herself inside for the remainder of her shift.

The general manager of The Sagamore, Mr. Thomas Guay, claims that he has never personally seen or experienced any of these phenomena. "I've worked here for over twenty years, and I've never seen a thing. I guess you could say I'm a self-avowed nonbeliever," said Guay. "I wouldn't mind experiencing something, just to say I'd seen it. And I've spoken to several guests who have had odd things take place during their stays. But I'm still waiting to see my first ghost."

The hotel provides a printed list of "Ghosts at the Sagamore" for guests to peruse. Anyone interested in staying at The Sagamore, for paranormal reasons or just for a wonderful vacation, can find information at https://www.thesagamore.com/.

ABANDONED VILLAGE AT WARDBORO

Some of the ghost villages found in the Adirondacks have been gone for so long that there really isn't much left to see, except perhaps a few stone wall foundations and perhaps an overgrown cemetery. One such deserted settlement is located near Bolton Landing, accessed by a dirt road leading into the canopied Adirondack forest. It is called Wardboro, and finding it requires some knowledge of the local area.

Gravestone of John Tanner in Wardboro Cemetery.

Photo by Larry Weill

The road to the site, which is just passable at best, used to connect the towns of Bolton and Hague. It was constructed sometime in the 1850s (or possibly earlier) and passes by numerous remains of this ancient, abandoned community.

One of the earliest settlers in this region was a man named John Tanner, who was born in 1778 and moved to the area outside of Bolton in 1818. He was a very industrious individual who raised a large family (14 children from his first two marriages alone) and successfully farmed a large tract of land off the shores of Lake George that eventually became known as Wardboro.

Tanner resided in the area for many years and appears to have been the driving force behind much of the local industry and economy. It is known that he owned and operated a large hotel, while also overseeing the operations of a farm that produced livestock and dairy products. His holdings also included sawmills and gristmills, although no traces of these remain today.

At the peak of its growth in the 1850s, Wardboro had approximately 23 homes, in addition to a school and numerous businesses. However, the population began to shrink in the following decade as the lumber business declined and the population migrated westward in search of soil that was more conducive to farming. The post office closed in 1867, marking the end of the community's organized structure.

While visiting this site, it is worth the time and effort to stop at the aging, abandoned cemetery and walk around the tombstones. In addition to the many Wards buried there, the gravestone of John Tanner still stands and can be easily located in the relatively small plot of ground.

Rock walls in the woods providing a viewing portal into the history of Wardboro.
PHOTO BY LARRY WEILL

Caution: If you decide to walk around the cemetery, which has been overrun with long grass and weeds, check yourself for ticks, which have become prevalent at this site.

To find the remains of Wardboro today, follow US Route 9N north through the town of Bolton Landing. Continue on US 9N past Northwest Bay, passing signs that note "Northwest Bay" on the right side of the road. Shortly after a small road, Padanarum Road, heads into the woods on the left. Take that left turn onto Padanarum and follow it to a fork in the road. Turn right onto Wardboro Road. (Padanarum Road continues off to the left.) Wardboro Road leads to the ghost village. Look for stone wall remains (previous photo) within the first few miles or for the historic marker near the Wardboro Cemetery.

THE LITTLE LIBRARY MADE FROM STONES

The Heintzelman Library building was not on our original list of attractions to review. However, as tourists pass through the tiny hamlet of Lake Brant in the community of Horicon, almost everyone's attention is diverted by the little stone building that stands directly on the southern shoreline of Brant Lake. The entire

Heintzelman Library, on the southern shoreline of Brant Lake.
PHOTO BY LARRY WEILL

building is composed of stones, the very same stones that form the base of the waterfront.

The Horicon Free Library was initially proposed by Mrs. Emily Heintzelman, a local property owner in the Brant Lake area, who mobilized both local residents and tourists alike to donate to the cause. The building was completed in 1907 and was stocked with books under the direction of Mrs. Heintzelman. As the library's primary benefactor, she continued to raise funds for additional volumes and donated numerous books she had acquired herself.

The building itself is most impressive in that it is comprised almost entirely of small, rounded stones that appear to have been smoothed by the waters of the lake. The doors, window frames, and roof are made of wood, but everything else is formed from stone, which gives the building a very primitive appearance. The words "Heintzelman Library 1907" are formed using smaller pebbles in an arch that extends beneath the peaked roof facing the street (NY Route 8).

The building served as the town's main library until 2001, when the collection of books outgrew the walls of the facility. The following year, the town constructed its new Horicon Town Community Center, which would double as its new and expanded library. Once the new library opened, the library's main collection was moved into the new building, and the Heintzelman Library was converted to house the local historical society. It also remains home to many volumes dedicated to the local area's historical records.

An interesting marble obelisk sits outside the Heintzelman Library commemorating the 150th anniversary of the founding of the town of Horicon. Erected in 1988, it proclaims "the creation of the Town of Horicon from the Town of Bolton Landing and Hague, on March 29, 1838."

The original Heintzelman Library building can be found by following Route 8 a little more than 2 miles from Route 87 (also known as the Adirondack Northway). The building sits directly on the left verge of the lightly traveled road, and parking is available at a small church across the street (assuming it is not in use).

BURIAL PLOT OF THE AREA'S EARLIEST DOUBLE AGENT

Harrisena Cemetery is a small plot of ground located next to the community church on US Route 9L outside of Lake George. Like many small burial grounds in this part of the state, many of the stones are engraved with the same last names, marking prominent families that homesteaded the area and were founding members of their respective churches.

Tombstone of Moses Harris, who died on November 13, 1838, at 89 years of age.
PHOTO BY LARRY WEILL

One of the more common names in this cemetery is Harris, as the Harris family moved into the region from Connecticut in the middle of the 1700s. Moses Harris was a military-minded young man who enlisted in the 5th Regiment of Dutchess County, thus commencing a period of service that would culminate in the tumultuous years of the Revolutionary War. His first several enlistments, each of which lasted for a period of one year, were all in different regiments and served under different commanders.

The historical record on Sergeant Moses Harris is not well recorded, and no likeness of him (painting or otherwise) can be found in any documents. However, it has been written that during his fourth enlistment, in 1777, Harris was serving in the area around Lake George when he found himself mixed in with a group of soldiers who were loyal to the king of England. They apparently thought that he shared their loyalty to the Crown; being desperately weakened from fleeing from American Colonists who were fighting against the troops loyal to the British Crown, they passed Harris a number of secret documents to transport to the English attaché in Albany.

Sergeant Harris took the letters, as requested, and carried them instead to General Philip Schuyler, who commanded the Northern American Army in Schuylerville. The letters, once opened, detailed the Loyalists' planned attack on Fort Stanwix, a key strategic point of defense for the Patriots along the Mohawk River Valley. Other letters in the cache handed to Harris contained plans for General Burgoyne and General Howe to attack the Patriots' territories in New York State.

The warnings provided by Sergeant Harris were passed to General George Washington and eliminated the chances of a successful surprise attack on Fort Stanwix. Harris was further utilized as a "double agent" to carry letters with fake war plans to General Carleton, governor of Canada. These duplicitous documents outlined a fake Patriot invasion of Canada, for which the Loyalists would have to arrange a defense using additional forces that would otherwise have been part of the army invading New York.

Harris served honorably through 1781, when he received an honorable discharge and commenced his civilian life. He returned to his home near Queensbury, New York, and lived another 57 years. There is some conflicting information regarding his date of death, as some references list it as November 13, 1837, while the date engraved on his tombstone reads November 13, 1838. However, if his lifespan was truly 89 years, then this would favor the 1838 date.

His tombstone is easy to find in the Harrisena Cemetery, which is located at 1616 Ridge Road, Queensbury, New York (Ridge Road is also US 9L). The graveyard is approximately 1 mile north of NY Route 149, on the right side of the road. Parking is available in the lot next to the church, which sits to the left side of the cemetery.

GHOSTS IN THE CHOCOLATE FACTORY

What could be better than a combination of handmade chocolate and skin-crawling ghost stories? You can actually get both of these attractions in one stop when you visit Barkeater Chocolates in North Creek, New York.

Barkeater Chocolates factory in North Creek.
PHOTO BY LARRY WEILL

12

Barkeater Chocolates is the brainchild of Jim and Debbie Morris, who originally operated their business using space in a café on Main Street in North Creek. They moved to their current location after purchasing the building in 2013.

"The building has stood here for nearly 150 years," said Debbie Morris. "It was built in the early 1880s, and the first deed on file is from 1884. It was owned by the Rexford family, where it passed from Samuel Rexford to his daughter-in-law Rebecca Rexford for the sum of $50.00. She in turn rented it out to tourists, who stayed in the various small rooms that then existed in the early days of the structure."

The building has gone through some rather tumultuous times since its construction, including having owners with "less than stellar reputations" (including one who married his mistress as his second wife, after which she mysteriously vanished) and a six-year-old child who was killed under suspicious circumstances. In later years, there were also two owners who died inside the house, although those deaths appear to have been due to natural causes.

According to Debbie Morris, they knew of nothing unusual about the house when they purchased it and moved in with their business. In those early days, there was no store set up in the building, just the space where they made

Factory and store of Barkeater Chocolates in North Creek.
Photo by Larry Weill

their chocolates and a makeshift office. Almost immediately after moving in, they began to experience unusual sounds and other phenomena.

"I was working in our little office one morning when I heard a person walk through the building, and then I started hearing some banging noises coming from the back," said Debbie. "But that didn't bother me because I knew one of our workers was coming in about that time, and we often make banging noises as we break apart our large batches of chocolate. But then, after no one stopped up to say hello, I walked to the back room and discovered it was empty; our employee had not yet arrived for the day!"

Morris states that soon afterward the employee reported for work, and she immediately questioned her about the noises she'd been hearing. The worker confirmed that she had not been present in the building, but also admitted that she had heard similar noises in the past few weeks without ever seeing anyone else around.

The supernatural phenomena witnessed inside the Barkeater facility include bags of chocolate "bark" flying off the shelf and striking the front wall, a distance of 3–4 feet. This has been witnessed a number of times, along with

Front of Barkeater Chocolates store, where bags of chocolate bark have been seen flying off the shelf toward the front wall.

Photo by Larry Weill

electronic door chimes sounding when the door was closed and locked. Other employees in the building have heard footsteps coming from upstairs when there was no one up there.

While the ghost stories have made for an amusing footnote to this charming Adirondack story, the focus should probably rest on the chocolate itself, which is absolutely delicious. I decided that I had to "quality check" several of the chocolates produced by Barkeater. After sampling the cherry chocolate bark and several of the truffles, I decided that I was most certainly a fan of their products. My guess is that the ghosts are as well.

Barkeater Chocolates is located at 3235 NY-28, North Creek, New York. The phone number is 518-251-4438. Check their hours of operation at https://barkeaterchocolates.com.

CARNIVALS CAN BE FUN AT -10°

All too often, the inhabitants of places like Upstate New York tend to go into hibernation when the snow starts flying. The drifts get deeper, the ice gets thicker,

Banner announcing the Brant Lake Winter Carnival.
Photo by Larry Weill

and the mercury at the bottom of the thermometer retreats into a little ball at the bottom of the glass. Under such extreme conditions, only the hardiest skiers and the most thick-blooded ice fishermen venture out to face the elements.

In 2011, residents and community businessmen of Brant Lake decided to do something about this problem. Other Adirondack communities had sponsored winter festivals attracting thousands of visitors, so why couldn't they? And so, with a couple of ideas and a vision of what could be, this small hamlet on the northern edge of Warren County decided to make their dream a reality.

"The initial idea was to start a family-oriented event that was fun, and also free," said Rob Olson, a member of the local town council and avid supporter of the annual Brant Lake Winter Carnival. "It started out fairly small, with perhaps only a hundred or so people showing up. But it's continued to grow every year, and now we have at least ten times that attending every year."

The prime organizing force behind the festival was a group originally called the Businessman's Alliance, which was later restructured and renamed the Tri-Lakes Community Alliance. This not-for-profit association of volunteers has organized business owners, families, and local citizens into a thriving entity that has taken on projects such as the Winter Carnival for the betterment of the entire area and its residents.

The Brant Lake Winter Carnival makes use of the facilities of Jimbo's Club at the Point, which originated as a rustic Adirondack camp for girls. Throughout the years, it has developed into a first-class club and dining facility that hosts

Human foosball game in action at the Brant Lake Winter Carnival, 2020. Jimbo's main buildings can be seen in the background.
Photo by Larry Weill

numerous events throughout the year. It has served as the local sponsor for the Winter Festival since 2012.

Brandon Himloff, who is the son of Jimbo's owner, also serves as chair of the Winter Carnival committee. "Part of what we're trying to do is to bring the small town back to the small town," Himloff explains. "It's all about family and community, and bringing our strengths in this community together."

Himloff has worked with a small but dedicated band of volunteers to keep interest in this event growing with each passing year. The cochair of the event, Cindy Meade, is a tireless enthusiast who seems to be everywhere at the same time. "She's the real driving force of the Winter Carnival" said Himloff. "Without her energy and passion, we'd have a tough time pulling this off."

The carnival includes many games, sports, and competitions, many of which are unique to the Adirondacks. The more traditional events include such diverse activities as ice hockey, curling, ice bowling, broomball, and a snowshoe race. Some of the more unusual contests include the Frying Pan Toss and the ever-popular Outhouse Race, in which competitors push outhouses mounted on skis down an ice track on the lake. (A separate story on this event follows.)

The festivities of the day are followed by an awards ceremony, then concluded with a fireworks display in the evening. Food is available throughout the

Volunteers clear snow off the ice to prepare a makeshift hockey "arena" for the Brant Lake Winter Carnival.
Photo by Larry Weill

day from a local Boy Scout troop, whose members provide hot dogs, hamburgers, bowls of chili, and other tasty treats for those who wish to dine outdoors.

"We thought about having commercial vendors come in with mobile kitchen trucks," said Himloff. "But then we decided that this should be all about the local community groups like the Boy Scouts and Cub Scouts, and helping their cause. They've done a really good job of keeping up with the demand, and we're proud to have them here serving our local residents."

The volunteers who coordinate the annual event do an amazing job of coping with the challenges that arise each year. "You never can tell what you're going to have to deal with," said Cindy Meade. "One year, the weather warmed up and we were up to our ankles in water on the ice. But we're Adirondackers who are used to adversity, and we haven't met an obstacle yet that we couldn't conquer."

For more on the Brant Lake Winter Carnival, visit http://www.trilakes alliance.com/events-activities/brant-lake-winter-carnival for additional information and schedule dates. If you do decide to attend, please dress for the occasion, as temperatures can often dive well below zero. But "warm-up" facilities are provided, and the fun is definitely worth the effort. Be sure to check the status of the carnival online before attending, as the event was canceled in 2024 due to lack of ice, which may happen again in the future.

The next two entries describe events that are both part of the Brant Lake extravaganza.

ADIRONDACK OUTHOUSES . . . ON SKIS?

Another iconic feature commonly seen across the Adirondack Park is the outhouse. A reminder of days gone by, the outhouse is still in use in remote, hard-to-reach areas where neither sewer systems nor septic tanks have yet to extend their reach.

Outhouses have taken on a virtually endless array of shapes and sizes throughout the years, from the small and cramped to the large and whimsical. However, those brought to the Brant Lake Winter Carnival every year have but one requirement: They need to be fast.

The annual Outhouse Race has become one of the favorite events in the annual festival, attracting not only a slew of racing teams but also hundreds of spectators, who line the course for the individual heats. "It's fun, it's unusual, and it's always good for a laugh," said JoAnne Morelli, a Schenectady resident visiting for the day. "An outhouse traveling at 15 miles per hour across a frozen lake just isn't something we see every day back home."

Competing teams sprinting down the ice in the 2020 Outhouse Race at the Brant Lake Winter Carnival.

Photo by Larry Weill

The Outhouse Race is one of the main drawing cards at the Brant Lake Winter Carnival and now draws a field of six to eight competing teams. These competitors use their skill and imagination to design and build rustic works of art that are then mounted on snow skis. The object is to make them as light and fast as possible so they can be propelled down the ice to the finish line.

"This is all about fun and community involvement," said several members of the Horicon Volunteer Fire Department. "We've been doing this race for three years now, and we just have a blast. Not much else goes on in the winter around here, so this gives us a chance to get out and be with all our friends from the community." Of the 22 members of the local fire department, 6 were present for the festival, 5 of whom would participate in the race.

The race course is only 100 feet long, although it appears much longer in person. The goal is obviously to build an outhouse racer that is as light as possible, with "fast" skis that reduce the friction as much as possible. The rules allow each team to have four people pushing and require that one person be sitting inside the outhouse "on the throne." How appropriate!

If you decide to attend this event, be sure to wear plenty of warm clothing in layers. The day of the 2020 carnival began with a temperature reading of –10°, so be prepared!

THE GREAT ADIRONDACK FRYING PAN TOSS

Truly accomplished cooks of the Adirondack logging camps were well known for supposedly flipping pancakes from the frying pan so high that people standing outside the cabin could watch the cake come out the top of the chimney, take a turn or two above the cabin, then fall back down the chimney, where the cook would expertly catch it back in the pan. Or so the legend goes.

Festivalgoers at the Brant Lake Winter Carnival were interested in a different kind of toss at the annual event: the throwing of a heavy pan *without* the food inside. It's become a staple event in a number of Adirondack winter carnivals and one of the more popular contests at the Brant Lake celebration.

"We've done this event every year for at least the last 7–8 years," said Cindy Meade, who serves as cochair of the carnival committee and can be seen everywhere throughout the duration of the festivities. "It's just another one of those fun things that gets everyone involved. I mean, who can't throw a frying pan?"

Contestant in the Frying Pan Toss competition throwing a heavy pan in early rounds of the contest.
Photo by Larry Weill

20

The truth of the matter is, not everyone is capable of sending these hefty cooking devices flying far enough to compete for the top honors. They are actually quite heavy, with the largest ones (used for the adult male competition) weighing in somewhere around 8–10 pounds.

"Although cast iron is the material of choice for frying pans, we can't use those for the throwing event," stated Meade. "Cast iron often breaks when it impacts the ground in really frigid conditions. So we use steel pans, which tend to hold up better."

The rules for the contest are actually fairly simple, including that contestants use an underhand throw and take care to avoid hitting any bystanders. However, the "official rules" posted nearby provide a litany of comic requirements, including the exclusion of steroid use, the absence of food in the pan, and also that "decapitation of any spectator is grounds for disqualification."

While the event is conducted purely in fun, some of the contestants achieved remarkable distances with their throws. The farthest toss in the men's division measured at 91 feet 6 inches, while the women's champion reached more than 57 feet.

The people participating in this event were an evenly mixed group of local residents and visiting tourists. "We're having a blast here" said Carl Barlow, a resident of nearby Chestertown, New York. "I was born here, but it's my first year attending the Brant Lake Winter Carnival. For me, it's all about getting the kids out of the house and into the great outdoors. They're having lots of fun, and it's free. That's a great combination."

The Frying Pan Toss is an annual part of the winter carnival, and everyone is welcome. For more information on the event visit http://www.trilakesalliance .com/events-activities/brant-lake-winter-carnival.

THE END OF THE HOWARD JOHNSON'S ERA

There are a great many people out there who have never eaten at a Howard Johnson's restaurant, especially if they are on the younger side of 30. Sadly, for those who never had that opportunity, it is gone forever with the closing of the last surviving "HoJo's" restaurant, which was located in Lake George, New York. It shut its doors for the last time in March 2022, marking the end of an era.

Howard Johnson's was more than a restaurant to much of the American public. With its landmark orange roof and blue cupola topped with the ubiquitous weather vane, it was an iconic part of Americana. There was little need for a sign in front of the restaurant, as everyone knew and instantly recognized the color scheme. It was unmistakable.

Photo of the Howard Johnson's restaurant in Lake George, prior to its closing in 2022.
PHOTO BY LARRY WEILL

The first Howard Johnson's business was launched in 1925 by Howard Deering Johnson. It wasn't really a restaurant as much as a drugstore that also sold ice cream. The owner quickly realized that the ice cream was the most successful part of his business, and he improved on the quality and expanded the number of flavors. Howard Johnson's "28 flavors" became its most famous calling card to advertise the chain and bring in new customers.

Howard Johnson's business expanded greatly through the 1930s and 1940s, attracting families up and down the East Coast to its large and varied menu and its informal dining rooms. The chain went through several expansions and contractions through the 1970s, when it reached its peak at more than 1,000 locations. (This included both franchised and independently owned restaurants.)

The chain eventually fell on hard times due to numerous ownership and economic factors. However, the Adirondacks were home to a few of the last surviving locations. The author of this book dined frequently at the location in Lake Placid, New York, while working there during the 1980 Winter Olympics.

For those diners who were devoted to Howard Johnson's menu, it boasted a number of items that were inextricably linked to the chain. One favorite of the author was the unique Clam Boat, which consisted of a load of golden-fried clam

Counter seating inside the front of the Lake George Howard Johnson's restaurant.
Photo by Larry Weill

strips loaded into a toasted long bun. The accoutrements included the almost-mandatory French fries and a healthy heap of coleslaw.

My last visit to the Lake George location was in August 2020. Already the patronage had fallen off to almost zero, and the writing was on the wall regarding the coming closure. I spoke to the manager at the time, who expressed regrets about the difficulty keeping the restaurant open. Still, for those who spent late nights under the orange roof consuming fried clams and other famous menu items, it will all be seriously missed. The empty restaurant still sits vacant along the west side of US Route 9, It was at 2143 State Route 9, Lake George, New York, a visual reminder of our past that is gone forever.

BLOODY POND: A GHASTLY SIGHT

The stark blue historical marker sign with yellow lettering is succinct. Unlike many historical signs with similar intent that provide a paragraph of details, this one consists of only two words with ten letters, followed by a date:

Bloody Pond. 1755.

Historic sign marking the location of Bloody Pond, which is not easily seen from the road.

PHOTO BY LARRY WEILL

The name conjures up a grisly image from another, more barbaric time when soldiers faced off in hand-to-hand combat, and hundreds (if not thousands) lost their lives in a single skirmish. The history of the battle dates back to the French and Indian War, predating the American Revolution by two decades.

According to historical accounts, it was on this spot, on September 8, 1755, that warring members of the Provincial Regiments of New York and New Hampshire engaged enemy troops from Britain and Canada allied with Native American warriors. The ensuing battle took the lives of several hundred men. The bodies of these soldiers were simply rolled into the pond at the bottom of the slope and left to rot. Legend has it that the

Bloody Pond, as viewed from the side of US Route 9 south of Lake George.

PHOTO BY LARRY WEILL

presence of the mutilated corpses actually stained the water red, the origin of the pond's name.

For history buffs and others, including tourists weary from shopping the many outlet stores in the area, Bloody Pond is an easy and accessible place to visit. Driving on US Route 9 from Queensbury to Lake George, the sign is easily seen as you approach the Magic Forest theme park. "Magic Forest" is now operating as "Lake George Expedition Park." The street address is 1912 US 9, Lake George, New York. The pond itself is not readily visible through the trees and vegetation, but there is a path leading from the road down to the water. A monument marking the location is also found at the bottom of the hill, within a minute's walk of the road.

Additional details about the battle are engraved on a metal plaque mounted on a boulder near the historic marker. It contains facts regarding the key military leaders in the fight as well as the makeup of the opposing forces.

This sight, while not worth a separate trip, is easily included when touring the Lake George Battlegrounds Park and other local eighteenth-century points of interest. There is no entry fee, and the location is accessible all day long.

Monument next to Bloody Pond marking the site where 200–300 soldiers lost their lives during the French and Indian War.
PHOTO BY LARRY WEILL

25

NORTH CREEK RAILWAY DEPOT MUSEUM

The history of the Adirondack region is rich with a number of railway systems and museums, some of which are described in this book. However, none of these are as ingrained in the history of our region and indeed in the annals of our country as the North Creek Railway Depot.

The station was built in 1872 and sits in the hamlet of North Creek, which is part of the town of Johnsburg. The station's primary claim to fame dates back to the assassination of President William McKinley and the ensuing inauguration of President Theodore "Teddy" Roosevelt. Roosevelt was at an event on Lake Champlain on September 6, 1901, when he learned that McKinley had been shot. After traveling to Buffalo and being reassured that the president would probably survive, he returned to the Adirondacks and was camping on Mount Marcy when he was located by messengers with grave news: McKinley was now on his deathbed and was not expected to survive the week.

Roosevelt did not wait for morning. He hustled out of the woods and risked a dangerous, high-speed horse-and-carriage ride over dark Adirondack roads to reach the train depot at North Creek. There, he received the news that McKinley had indeed passed away that morning, and that he would be inaugurated as the

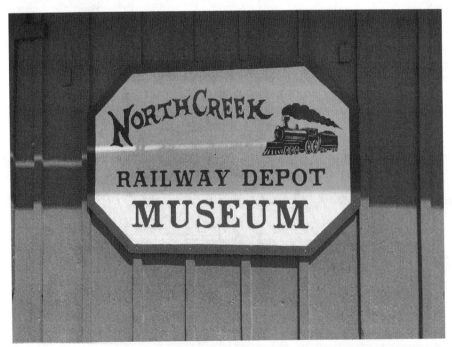

Sign on the front wall of the North Creek Railway Depot Museum.
PHOTO BY LARRY WEILL

twenty-sixth president of the United States. The North Creek Railway Depot will forever be known as the location where Roosevelt learned that he would be the next president and from where he began his historic trip to the ceremony in Buffalo.

The North Creek Railway Depot has been converted into a wonderful museum for sightseers to view the long history of the North Creek and Saratoga Railroads. The exhibits explain the contributions made by the railway in transporting many of the region's resources, including garnet, tannery supplies, and iron ore. Many other rail systems (e.g., the Lake Ontario and Hudson River Railroad Company) operated in conjunction with the North Creek, and their stories can be found here as well.

Located at 5 Railroad Pl, North Creek, New York, the museum is open every year from June through Labor Day. Hours may vary based on the month and day of the week, so call or visit the website at https://www.northcreek depotmuseum.com for specific details. One of the more attractive features of the museum is that it does not charge an entry fee. However, donations are greatly appreciated and help to support the facility.

Interpretive exhibit of historical railroad routes and photographs at the North Creek Railway Depot Museum.
Photo by Larry Weill

In addition to the train depot and grounds (including an engine house, full-sized turntable, and other structures), there are many other attractions to interest sightseers in the North Creek area. Numerous shops, restaurants, and other facilities are situated around the small town, as well as activities such as Garnet Mine tours, picnic areas, flyfishing schools, and "railbike" rides. Plan on spending at least one full day to take in all the sights.

WHERE'S THAT CONFOUNDED BRIDGE?

Depending on the source consulted, the number of bridges in the United States is somewhere between 614,000 and 618,000. That's a lot of bridges, and they include structures of all kinds, lengths, and materials. One of these bridges, how-ever, is not man-made and is wonderfully different from all the others.

Located in the hamlet of Pottersville, New York, in Warren County on the southwest side of Schroon Lake, is the marvelous geologic attraction known as Natural Stone Bridge & Caves.

Entrance to the cave system beneath the marble stone bridge at Natural Stone Bridge & Caves.

Photo by Larry Weill

This attraction is billed as the "largest marble cave entrance in the Eastern United States." It is located on private land that has been in the owner's family for more than 200 years. The owners have developed the land to maximize access and viewing for visitors of all ages, with a plethora of options regarding the level of activity and the types of events available.

Unlike many of the attractions in this book, Natural Stone Bridge & Caves is widely known and well advertised and has been part of Adirondack visitors' vacation itineraries for many decades. It is great for families, as it includes an easy-to-follow trail system that walks tourists through the grounds and explains the many features of the geological panorama in easy-to-understand terms. The walkways are well constructed and safe for almost anyone, although care must be taken with some features (i.e., short overhead ceilings and rock protrusions) that are part of the landscape.

Numerous tours are offered by the facility, providing opportunities for walking, spelunking, and even submerged "cave crawls" through sand, mud, and water. Adventure Tours are advertised specifically for those in good physical condition who can maneuver freely in tight conditions. For those who want to tackle

One of the many log and plank walkways that transects the Natural Stone Bridge & Caves site.

Photo by Larry Weill

the full experience inside the cave system, read the full web page regarding what to wear and expect on the tour.

For those who are a bit less adventurous, the facility offers an entire program full of other activities, which even include disc golf. (Think frisbees!) Individuals can enjoy winter hikes on snowshoes, as well as self-guided hikes, and hiking access to Catamount and Green Hill. The possibilities are endless. Note that the main trail through the site is about 0.75 mile in length and contains about 500 steps, many of which are irregular in height, so please take care and supervise any children who may be with you.

Many of the activities and tours listed on the website require special access and tickets, which may be reserved online. Make sure to visit https://stone bridgeandcaves.com for more information or to reserve a spot in your desired tour. The self-guided tour is $20.00 for adults and $10.00 for youth ages five to twelve. Children age four and under are free. Pets are not allowed. Peak season is from June 20 through September 5, although many offseason activities are also available.

There are too many additional details to list here, so please make sure to check out the website, and then get ready to enjoy a wonderful day (or longer) with your family.

IS FORT WILLIAM HENRY HAUNTED?

Like many structures built in this country more than 200 years ago, Fort William Henry is not the original construction. The first fort was built at the southern end of Lake George in 1755 by British forces during the French and Indian War. They intended to use it as a launching point against the French-built Fort Saint-Frédéric, at current-day Crown Point. However, the French attacked first in 1757 and laid siege to the fort, forcing the British forces to surrender.

The larger French force, under General Louis-Joseph de Montcalm, was accompanied by about 2,000 Native Americans of various tribes. Many of them ignored Montcalm's orders and participated in the slaughter of surrendered British soldiers as they retreated from the grounds, resulting in a bloody massacre. The estimated number of slain soldiers varies widely among sources, but most historians believe the figure to be somewhere around 200.

Throughout the years, a great many ghost stories have originated based on the bloody battle and ensuing carnage in and around the site. Battlefields across the country have shared this eerie connection, and Fort William Henry was one of the more macabre locations of the French and Indian War.

Front entry gate of Fort William Henry.
PHOTO BY LARRY WEILL

The facility, which was completely destroyed and abandoned for two centuries, was rebuilt in the 1950s. Local businessmen, seeking to recreate the historic structure as well as enhance local tourism, decided to construct a replica that was accurate in size and footprint to the original. The sides of the fort are roughly square in shape, with thick walls and reinforced bastions located on the corners. Inside the fort itself are a large number of display cases containing artifacts such as weapons, uniforms, and items of everyday use like mess utensils and other supplies.

Display of muskets inside hallway of Fort William Henry.
PHOTO BY LARRY WEILL

The fort is also replete with replica cannons, which are fired during demonstrations of the fortification's defenses. The guides who perform these demonstrations are dressed in period uniforms and are well versed in the history of the fort and its battle actions.

Located at 48 Canada Street, Lake George, New York, the Fort William Henry Museum is open limited hours offseason but is open daily after May 1. A variety of tours are available, including standard museum tours as well as specialized "ghost tours." Most adult tickets cost around $22.00, with discounts available for seniors, students, and children. Military personnel and veterans can gain access for free with a valid ID card.

Please note that this facility is not advertised as being "handicapped accessible," as there are many stairs and irregular surfaces to navigate throughout the structure. Ticket reservations are highly advised, as many tours and events are sold out several days in advance.

To contact the Fort William Henry Museum for more information or tickets, call 518-668-5471 or visit https://www.fwhmuseum.com.

LAKE GEORGE BATTLEFIELD PARK

Not every attraction in the Adirondacks is "bizarre or forgotten." If history is your thing, you will find yourself surrounded with more historic sites than can be visited in any reasonable-length vacation. This is certainly true in the area around Lake George, where many of the attractions and memorials are linked to one another through the early battles of our nation.

Statue of William Johnson and Mohawk King Hendrick at Lake George Battlefield Park.
PHOTO BY LARRY WEILL

One immediately obvious feature of this park's grounds is that it is filled with statues. They are all around you as you stroll along the paths. Most of these memorials have plaques describing the historical figures depicted. These include William Johnson and Mohawk King Hendrick (see previous picture), Saint Isaac Jogues (a Jesuit priest who was the first European to see Lake George), the Mohawk Warrior statue, and the Memorial to Four Unknown Soldiers. These statues commemorate battles and events over multiple wars and many decades of historical deeds, yet they are all colocated within a short walk of each other in this picturesque setting.

One great feature of this park is that it offers a lot more than just history. It is located on 35 acres of land at the southern end of Lake George, so it includes a nice length of waterfront property that can be used for family outings and picnics. There is a small fee to park in the lot, which is centrally located to all the park's other amenities, including picnic tables and BBQ grills, which are available for public use. There are also public bathrooms and water available on site. The entire park is operated by the New York State Department of Environmental Conservation (DEC).

Statue commemorating the life and work of Saint Isaac Jogues, the Jesuit priest who lived with the Hurons in New York in the seventeenth century.
Photo by Larry Weill

If you have a large group and need the use of a pavilion, two are available and can be rented for a reasonable fee. Pets are not permitted on the grounds, which is a rule that is consistent with other DEC day-use areas. Poison ivy has been observed in several locations throughout the park, so take care and recognize the characteristics of this toxic plant.

The park is located at the intersection of Fort George Road and Beach Road, Lake George, New York, and it is open 24 hours a day, 365 days a year. A nice self-guided tour brochure that describes all the statues and memorials in the park is available at https://extapps.dec.ny.gov/docs/permits_ej_operations_pdf/tourlgbattlefield.pdf.

CROWN POINT LIGHTHOUSE

By their very nature, lighthouses are unique and romantic structures. Always located on a coastline, they instantly invoke the image of the solitary lighthouse keeper steadfastly watching over the stormy waters surrounding the beacon. While most navigational lights are no longer manned, the structures remain a beloved part of our landscape and history.

One of the most picturesque and historic lighthouses on the eastern seaboard of the United States is located at Crown Point, New York. Still called a lighthouse, the structure that exists today is actually a monument to Samuel de Champlain, who was credited with "discovering" Lake Champlain during his explorations in 1609.

The Crown Point Lighthouse is very different from most similar structures in many ways. Its origins, composition, size, and evolution would fill an entire volume, although most of those details remain hidden to the average weekend sightseer. The original lighthouse, which

Crown Point Lighthouse, spring 2023.
PHOTO BY LARRY WEILL

first became functional in 1859, took the form of a simple octagonal stone tower. It was 55 feet in height and constructed of limestone blocks, with a window portal on top for the beacon. Attached to the lighthouse tower was a wooden residence for the family of the lighthouse keeper.

The magnificent upgrade of the lighthouse to its current form as a memorial was launched in 1910, when the structure was selected to serve as a commemoration of Samuel de Champlain's explorations and discovery of the lake that now bears his name. A design was selected that included a series of eight massive columns around the exterior. Ornate stone carvings adorn the upper surfaces, with the beacon room situated on top. A sculpture of Champlain with two other associates faces the other side of the edifice (facing the lake). A spiral staircase inside the interior of the structure is used to ascend to the observation room. Although still a "lighthouse," its construction and appearance far exceed its functional requirements.

While not officially inside the Adirondack Park, the lighthouse (as well as the nearby ruins) can be found within a few hundred yards of the Blue Line on the end of the peninsula that projects northeast into Lake Champlain just

Bronze plaque embedded in the base of the lighthouse as a tribute to Samuel de Champlain.

PHOTO BY LARRY WEILL

southeast of the Lake Champlain Bridge. It can be found on the Lighthouse Friends website, at https://www.lighthousefriends.com/light.asp?ID=672. The memorial can be accessed via a short walk from Bridge Road that runs through the historic site. There is a gateway at the entrance to the lighthouse road, although it was unoccupied at the time of the author's visit. Some visitors have reported having to pay a $3.00 entrance fee (even if not using the camping facilities), although this was not being enforced at the time of my visit.

The door at the base of the lighthouse that permits access to the stairway to the top is often left unlocked, although this was not the case during my visit. This is probably dependent on the season and the hour of the visit. Check the website for details.

HIGHLANDS CASTLE: THE CASTLE ON THE MOUNTAIN

Residents of the town of Bolton Landing, New York, are probably used to the sight. But anyone not familiar with the scenery of the area is bound to do a double-take ... and then a triple-take. The sight at the top of the mountain is so extraordinary and seemingly out of place that it defies logic, although it is very real.

Main Home castle at Highlands Castle on the mountain, Bolton Landing.
PHOTO COURTESY OF JOHN AND YVONNE LAVENDER

36

Highlands Castle is such an amazing and beautiful piece of construction that it defies words. Making it all the more incredible is that it is the brainstorm of a single man, John Lavender, who created the entire complex from a promise made to his three-year-old son in 1978. After going through a divorce at a young age, John promised his son that "someday I will build you a castle." Many individuals make extraordinary promises, but very few actually keep them. John Lavender is one of those very few people.

John found the property for his massive undertaking by pure coincidence after reading an advertisement in a local *Pennysaver* paper in 1982. With rare insight, he purchased the plot sight unseen and then set about developing it. He described his first visits to the top of the mountain, which required scrambling over rock ledges and massive boulders: "You really couldn't see anything of the lake (Lake George) below since the trees obstructed the entire view. So I lived in a tent that entire summer, clearing the trees and burning it all off. As I worked, the views kept getting better and better until a magical landscape appeared that was just unbelievable."

The following year (1983) he began construction on the site, starting with the Home castle building. Once the foundation was in place, John was able to get a suitable wooden frame up for the building within about three months. It wasn't yet a castle, but it did have a roof over it that permitted him to sleep on a real floor instead of his tent, which was a step up.

Front foyer inside the entrance of the Home castle.
PHOTO COURTESY OF JOHN AND YVONNE LAVENDER

The task of moving all the rocks for the exterior was a Herculean effort that required a great amount of sheer muscle power. For this work, John enlisted the help of some outsiders who shared his vision. Later on, when his son Jason was a teenager, he joined in the grunt work, along with several members of his high school football team. "Jason proved to be extremely adept in stonework" said John. "He went on to earn a degree in Architectural Engineering from Penn State, so maybe building the castle was an inspiration that led to his eventual career."

After completing the Home castle, John went on to build two other castle-like structures: the Gatehouse (in 1988) and the Castle Cottage (in 1995). However, along the way something else of great importance took place in John's life. He met Yvonne, his current wife and constant companion, whom he credits with "taking this pile of rocks and making it into a home." Yvonne has brought life and laughter into Highlands Castle, and it is rewarding to see the bonds they've formed as a couple as well as with the castle complex. "I'm good at envisioning things before I build them," said John. "I can see things three dimensionally before I start construction. But Yvonne is superb at knowing what will go where, as well as coordinating the colors and textures of rooms and fixtures. Somehow, she just knows how to fit it all together."

In the lower level of the Home castle, John acted out his wish to have a hidden passageway and bedroom suite. The resulting King's Suite is not only spacious and beautiful, but is completely hidden from view behind a fake bookcase. Only by pressing on the carved wooden piece of furniture in the right location will the "doors" swing open, allowing access to the rooms.

Fake bookcase serving as entrance to a concealed lower-level bedroom suite in the Home castle.

Photo courtesy of John and Yvonne Lavender

On top of everything else, the Lavenders have completed the amazing imagery inside these castles with period art, fixtures, suits of armor, and a plethora of antique furnishings. In some ways, John believes that fate led to their finding and acquiring some of the pieces, including a series of four Tiffany-created glass doors that grace the entrance to the "great hall."

Creativity. Beauty. Awesome size. Historic. Inspiring. All these terms apply. It has to be seen to be believed.

In 2010, John and Yvonne began sharing their home with the public, renting out the bedroom suites and the great hall on a private basis. People interested in this unique experience can view the rooms and availability on the website at https://highlandscastle.com. You can also reach them by phone at 518-796-9118.

Please note that this site is not open to the general public without a rental.

GANGSTER'S TREASURE IN THE ADIRONDACKS!

The Adirondacks are such a pure, pristine, and beautiful place that one never associates them with the criminal underworld. The very thought of the mountains and forests harboring a vicious killer is almost unfathomable. But that apparently happened.

The name of the gangster in question was Dutch Schultz, born Arthur Simon Flegenheimer. After enduring a rough childhood in a broken family, he entered a life of crime and was already incarcerated by the age of 17. After being released from jail in 1920, he immediately reentered the criminal world and formed partnerships with other felonious characters.

During the Prohibition Era, Schultz turned to operating illegal speakeasies and transporting millions of dollars of bootleg alcohol from Canada to the underground bars in New York. As his reputation and power grew, so did his taste for control and violence. He and a partner (Joey Noe) became embroiled in gang warfare that resulted in the deaths of many underworld figures.

Photo of Dutch Schultz, date unknown.
PUBLIC DOMAIN

Schultz went through many legal battles with the federal government, and he was also being pursued by powerful competing criminal gangs. By 1935, he foresaw his own end by either capture or assassination. Wishing to protect his personal fortune, reported to be $5–7 million, he had a specially constructed weatherproof safe box built in which he reportedly buried a vast "treasure" of bonds, cash, and gold. This he proceeded to bury in a remote location in either the Catskills or farther north, near a favorite resort of his in present-day Stony Creek, New York. The only person who was with Schultz when the treasure was buried was his bodyguard, Bernard "Lulu" Rosenkrantz.

Schultz's premonition proved to be true, and he died following a "hit" by rival mob members in a restaurant in Newark, NJ. Among the others killed with Schultz was Rosenkrantz, his bodyguard, who was the only other individual who knew the exact burial spot of the treasure.

Many people familiar with the story favor the Stony Creek location as the most probable location of the treasure. "One-by-one, they've eliminated most of the other suggested hiding places," said Denise Martin, one of the proprietors of The Lodge at Harrisburg Lake. "If you look at all the clues Schultz talked about while on his deathbed, it all makes sense."

Martin's partner in the business, Stuart Strzelczyk, also agrees with this theory: "Among the clues he left were that you could see the hiding place from the tallest elevation in the county. That spot, here in Saratoga County, is Tenant Mountain, and you can see The Lodge from its peak."

The original horse barn building at The Lodge, converted into a dance floor and party event room.
Photo by Larry Weill

Strzelczyk and Martin also pointed to the fact that Dutch Schultz enjoyed visiting the resort site (which was a dude ranch) to ride horses, which was one of his favorite pastimes. "The ranch was at the end of a long dead-end road, so he could keep a close eye on who came in and who left," said Martin. "Not only that, but the land was at the edge of the Wilcox Lake Wild Forest, so he could disappear into the woods if he needed to make a quick getaway. He even had a seaplane on Harrisburg Lake, so he could 'make tracks' in a hurry if the Feds showed up to arrest him."

Whether the treasure is really buried there today is a matter of debate and speculation. There are differing reports about what Schultz whispered in his dying moments, assuming that there was any credence to his last words. Assuming that the treasure is real, and that it still survives intact, it would be worth $55–70 million today. That is enough to have attracted a major television travel show and with a nationally known treasure hunting specialist. Their visits failed to turn up any concrete evidence that the safe box is still buried in the ground at Stony Creek, although conducting a comprehensive search would take years. Still, the story and the myth are irresistible legends that have become an integral part of folklore at The Lodge at Harrisburg Lake.

Today, Denise Martin and Stuart Strzelczyk run The Lodge at Harrisburg Lake, located at 1200 Harrisburg Road, Stony Creek, New York, as a wonderful rental property for family reunions, weddings, and other large gatherings. They don't rent individual rooms, but instead offer the entire 6,000-square-foot lodge (along with the outer buildings) for large, memorable family gatherings. "We didn't know how this was going to go when we opened for business back in 2015. But today, our lodge is booked a full year in advance," said Martin. "We offer families a truly unique facility; a lodge, dining area, bar, dance floor and gym, and countless activities to make their truly once-in-a-lifetime affairs."

Stuart Strzelczyk and Denise Martin, proprietors of The Lodge at Harrisburg Lake, standing outside their magnificent facility in Stony Creek, New York.

Photo by Larry Weill

View into the dining room of The Lodge at Harrisburg Lake.
PHOTO BY LARRY WEILL

The Lodge at Harrisburg Lake is available for reunions and weddings (and other events) for multiple days, if desired. The property includes 66 acres of beautiful meadows and forests. An enjoyable time is almost certainly guaranteed, although finding the treasure is not.

For more information about The Lodge at Harrisburg Lake, visit the website at https://www.thelodgehlreunionretreat.com or call 518-696-4944.

AN ADIRONDACK WOOF STOCK: IT'S ALL ABOUT THE DOGS

Woof Stock. No, that's not a typo. Woodstock took place in August 1969 and was all about the music (among other less reputable things). Woof Stock has become an annual event in Warren County, and it's all about the dogs.

The event organizer for Woof Stock is Cindy Mead, a semiretired real estate broker who has owned her own business since 1995. Many years ago, she got together with a number of other local businesspeople and decided to organize events that would bring people to town.

"Woof Stock is now in its eighth year," said Mead, "and it's been growing every year. We usually get more than 2,000 people attending, along with about 1,000 dogs. About 80–90 percent of the people who show up bring their dogs along with them, so it's become a pretty big thing."

The event is based in Chestertown, behind the town hall building at 6307 US-9, Chestertown, New York. The large field is filled with a variety of vendors offering food and merchandise, much of which is geared toward the canines. There are also various shows and events scheduled throughout the day, many of which involve trained dogs who have been brought by the exhibitors.

The festival also includes Lure Coursing, Costume Contests, K9 Demos, and a Blessing of the Animals. "One of the favorites is the 'dock diving' event," said Mead. "It's a traveling show company that sets up a large diving tank at the end of a straight running track. The dogs sprint down the track and launch themselves into the water, where their jumps are measured and scored. It always attracts a crowd."

Another great function of Woof Stock is to provide a recruiting spot for organizations like Guiding Eyes, which raises puppies who will eventually serve as seeing eye dogs for the visually impaired. "We are always looking for puppy raisers," said Gary, who represents the nonprofit organization. "Only about one dog in three successfully completes the full training period and is placed with a recipient, so there is a constant need for these people."

Many of the visitors to Woof Stock said they've been coming for years,

Woof Stock mascot (Chester) offering doggy kisses at the kissing booth.
PHOTO BY LARRY WEILL

Gary, a puppy-raiser from Guiding Eyes, speaks to the public about the seeing-eye dog program.
PHOTO BY LARRY WEILL

although several others mentioned it was their first visit. Steven and Kathy, of Queensbury, New York, said it was their first time attending. "Our little Bichon Frisé (named Lilly) is 15 years old, and completely deaf," said Steve. "We're just trying to take her places so that she can enjoy the last years of her life."

Other organizations, including the SPCA, are represented at Woof Stock and attract their share of attention. Weslie, an Albany resident attending Woof Stock for the first time, is planning on adopting a dog through the SPCA. "We lost our dog about eight years ago, and our daughter has been asking us to adopt a replacement ever since."

Woof Stock also dedicates a portion of the weekend to music-related activities, with live bands playing on the field throughout the day on both Saturday and Sunday.

"It's like bringing your dog to the carnival," said Cindy Mead.

The event is billed as "a weekend of Peace, Paws, and Music." "Come up to Chestertown and see us next year. We'd love to see you *and* your dogs!" https://www.facebook.com/adirondackwoofstock/.

WE ALL SCREAM FOR ICE CREAM

The iconic Martha's rooster sign, which sits in front of the famous ice cream stand on US Route 9 in Queensbury.
PHOTO BY LARRY WEILL

The purpose of this guidebook is to focus on the forgotten and unusual attractions of the Adirondacks rather than discuss locations to eat or access lodging. But there is one place, located just south of Lake George, that defies the ordinary. It is an iconic ice cream stand that attracts thousands of visitors every day, where being seen is just as important as the flavor of your ice cream cone.

The ice cream stand and restaurant have an interesting past, as recalled by Dennis LaFontaine, the current owner. LaFontaine said that the original owner was a woman named Martha Freiberger, who bought the original house on the property in the 1940s. This was during the period when the Adirondack Northway (Interstate 87) was under construction. They built a restaurant for the workers who were building the highway, which led them to construct the first parts of the current building. Martha's husband, Carl, added the first one-window ice cream stand in 1947. This was even before the start of Storytown USA, which was built across the street in 1954.

LaFontaine's family used to vacation at the amusement park across the street, and in 1982 they learned that Martha wanted to sell the business. One thing led to another, and the LaFontaines purchased Martha's place in 1983. Dennis was still living in Connecticut and helping to run the family's catering business while still a senior in high school, which was a huge responsibility for a teenager.

In 1983, Dennis moved to the Lake George area and took over food operations. In 1999, Six Flags bought the entire operation, and at one time considered razing the ice cream stand and restaurant to expand its own park. However, the company decided to leave it intact and, in 2009, sold the building and business back to LaFontaine, who has run it ever since.

"We come here every time we're in the area," said Joe and Laura, a couple visiting from Rockland County. "We're up to visit Magic Forest, but we *always* come to Martha's for ice cream every afternoon. Their serving sizes are HUGE, and the flavors are wonderful. Our two-year-old loves it too!"

Crowds forming in midafternoon. Lines at the ice cream stand become progressively longer as the evening approaches.
PHOTO BY LARRY WEILL

Dennis LaFontaine credits his business philosophy for the success of the establishment. "Every time someone comes to the window, we try to blow them out of the water with our products and our service." LaFontaine employs 80 people at the stand, and they all seem to radiate his friendly enthusiasm for outstanding service.

If you'd like to visit Martha's, there are two ways to find the place. The first is to go to 1133 US Route 9 in Queensbury. The second is to start driving up US 9 between Glens Falls and Lake George, then look for a huge crowd of happy people eating ice cream at a stand on the left side of the road. Either way will work.

Side note: To validate the quality of the product at Martha's, the author felt the need to sample a "small" cone of Dole Cherry ice cream. It was piled 6 inches above the cone, and definitely lived up to its reputation!

LOTS TO FIND AT THE GARNET MINE!

Garnets are among the most famous minerals found in the Adirondacks. These are silicate minerals that have been treasured since the Bronze Age and used for both jewelry and their abrasive characteristics, in sandpaper.

Pit no. 1 of nine excavated pits at the Garnet Mine in North Creek.
PHOTO BY LARRY WEILL

While the geology and chemical composition of these crystalline minerals is beyond the scope of this book, the Garnet Mine in North Creek is a fascinating and fun place to visit. It permits tourists to come face to face with the actual mined rock walls and to dig for as much of the stone as they care to carry home, although charges do apply for the stones removed.

The individual credited with first developing the mine was Henry Hudson Barton, who arrived from London around 1860 and discovered the garnets in 1887. After first gaining access to the mineral rights, he acquired the land in 1889 and commenced mining operations. The mines have greatly expanded throughout the years, and the abundance of high-grade garnet has ensured the viability of the business for more than 130 years.

Access to the mine is via a dirt road located approximately 5 miles from Route 28 on Barton Mines Road. The road winds through green forests, climbing seemingly forever upward on the side of the mountain. It finally reaches a clearing where a gate prevents access until the start of the next tour. The clearing is also the site of the Gore Mountain Gem & Mineral Shop, currently owned and operated by Jason Brown.

Jason Brown, owner of the Gore Mountain Gem & Mineral Shop, inside his store.
PHOTO BY LARRY WEILL

"It's really been a family affair for almost four decades," said Brown. "My mother, Judy Brown, ran the shop for many years until they moved away 37 years ago. My father, Joe Brown, was the mineral cutter. We returned here in July of 2022, and have enjoyed working the gem shop once again. My parents, who are now both in their 70s, are both still involved on a part-time basis."

People enjoy visiting the mine for a variety of reasons. The tour offered by the gem shop is extremely educational, and visitors have fun digging for gem-quality garnets. "This is our second time at the mine," said Kathy Carattini of Carlisle, Pennsylvania. "We were here five years ago with our grandchildren. We really enjoy finding places that are off the beaten path, and digging for these beautiful stones is a lot of fun."

Unlike other mines in the Adirondacks, which require a great amount of work to find stones, the garnets are easy to locate at North Creek. As Jason says, "Everyone will find something to bring home." The parking area literally sparkles with tiny garnet crystals, and much larger stones can be found with little effort using a digging trowel and screen.

For those so inclined, beautiful, cut stones can be found already made into stunning jewelry inside the gift shop. Many of these pieces come from stones brought out of the nearby mine. Prices are very reasonable, and the selection is extensive.

The tours, which are led by knowledgeable and friendly guides, are generally done three times a day: at 10:30 a.m., 12:30 p.m., and 3:00 p.m. They run from July 1 through Labor Day, with limited access during other warm-weather months. The tours are $18.00 for adults, $15.00 for seniors, and $10.00 for children. (Visitors are also charged a fee of $2.00/pound for garnets removed from the site.) Each visitor must drive their own vehicle from the gate to the mine (about 1 mile). An SUV is not required, as the road is very easy to navigate in a passenger car.

The Gore Mountain Gem & Mineral Shop can be found at 1126 Barton Mines Road, North Creek, New York. It can be reached by phone at 518-251-2706 or online at www.garnettours.net.

ATTRACTIONS OF HAMILTON COUNTY

GRAVESITE OF ADIRONDACK FRENCH LOUIE

Anyone who has ever hiked the remote trails of the West Canada Lakes Wilderness Area in Hamilton County is undoubtedly familiar with the legacy of Adirondack French Louie. One of the Adirondacks' most famous hermits, he made his home on the east side of West Lake (or "West Canada Lake") from the 1870s until the day before he died, on February 28, 1915.

French Louie's gravestone in the Speculator Cemetery.
PHOTO BY LARRY WEILL

49

Louie was a legendary hunter, trapper, and sometime guide in this section of woods, maintaining numerous camps and shacks on many of the lakes and waterways. Although he served as a willing host at his camps, he seldom interacted much with those who stayed with him. He was extremely independent and didn't want to be told what to do by anyone.

Louie's name is synonymous with this stretch of woods, and he was loved and adopted by the villagers of the town where he lived. (It was known as "Newtons Corners" prior to being renamed Speculator.) He was well known for his annual two-week visits to the town, during which he drowned his thirst with plentiful libations from the local pubs and barrooms.

Following his death in 1915, he was buried in a plot in a corner of the Speculator Cemetery, where he still rests today. His gravesite was improved by a group of "admirers" in 1954, when they placed a stone to mark his burial spot. Visitors to his grave still leave behind bottles of whiskey and other alcoholic beverages, in case Louie ever reemerges and seeks to whet his whistle. There is no street address for the cemetery. It is simply listed as "Elm Lake Road, Speculator." It is at the intersection of Route 30 and Elm Lake Road.

Louie was quite fond of saying that "he come back" after his death, so perhaps the gravesite and stone were unnecessary. However, to this date there have been no Louie sightings either in the woods or around town.

To find his grave, walk into the front entrance of the cemetery and turn left, then walk along the fence that borders Charlie John's Store. It is located about halfway toward the back of the cemetery, in a plot that sits right up against the fence.

French Louie's grave, in the first row against the fence, directly behind Charlie John's Store in Speculator.
PHOTO BY LARRY WEILL

PIG ROCK

Pig Rock is one of those strange sights that just seems to pop up in the middle of nowhere. Simply put, it is a large boulder that is crudely shaped like a pig and has been painted to accentuate those lines and call out the image. It's unmistakable, and everyone who lives within an hour's drive knows exactly what it is.

Located on NY Route 30 about 6 miles north of the town of Speculator, Pig Rock has been part of the landscape for a very long time. Back in the mid-1950s, Route 30 was a dirt road that connected Speculator to the town of Indian Lake farther north. When the state decided to pave the road, it first needed to widen the shoulders. It was during this work that Pig Rock was first discovered, although it was a "pig" in shape only as it was still unpainted. Since the boulder was already a local favorite, the work crews moved it farther back from the road to save it from demolition.

"A lot of the history of Pig Rock is a bit uncertain," said Aaron Weaver, the town of Lake Pleasant historian. "It's almost all 'oral history,' passed down from one generation to the next." According to Weaver, it was either local workers or members of Deerfoot Lodge who first painted the eyes and nose, just to make it stand out. This probably took place in the late 1950s or early 1960s.

Pig Rock, on NY Route 30, 6 miles north of Speculator.
Photo by Larry Weill

For some time, a friendly competition existed between the girl campers of Camp Tapawingo and the boy campers of Deerfoot Lodge. These two camps already competed in friendly sporting events, but the rivalry soon spread to include the painting of Pig Rock. The girls painted it pink, which prompted the boys to repaint it to the original gray.

Other individuals, whether campers or local residents, have had their fun with Pig Rock, adding features to keep it updated with current events. During the appearance of swine flu, a concerned individual covertly covered the Pig's snout with a mask. The effort must have worked, because Pig Rock did not contract the deadly virus.

Later on, in the 1990s, the state announced plans to expand Route 30 once again and intended to dynamite Pig Rock to enable the widening the lanes. However, the local citizens were having none of this. They vigorously protested the proposed work. Someone even went as far as painting a teardrop on the face of Pig Rock to represent the people's sentiments toward the bovine boulder. The state finally acquiesced and moved Pig Rock a second time, thus preserving Speculator's beloved natural statue.

Additional notes: Even though a great many interviews have been conducted with some of the older residents of Speculator, no one appears to have definitive knowledge of the first person(s) to paint Pig Rock. It was supposedly painted pink for at least some of the time in the 1970s. However, the author lived in this area from 1979 to 1981 and only recalls seeing it painted gray.

"GONE FISHING" IN PISECO

The stretch of highway along NY Route 8 near Piseco isn't known for its extraordinary works of art. It is more recognized for its dense stands of hemlock, spruce, and fir trees that line the edges of the road, punctuated only by the occasional turnoff or camp road. However, there is an exception to this rule, which has become familiar to visitors of the region for over a decade.

The carvings, which are approximately 12 feet tall, stand by the side of the road and greet travelers as they head toward the towns of Piseco and Lake Pleasant. While hundreds of cars pass by this site each day, very few people actually know the story behind these works of art and how they came to be.

The creator is Randy Huta, an enlightened college professor who arrived in Piseco in 1962. Huta had taught at Utica College for many years but had never used the camp at Piseco as his residence until after his retirement in 2001. A genuine Renaissance man, Huta admits that he created some of his first carvings as a way to entertain his grandchildren.

"Gone Fishing" carvings on NY Route 8 in Piseco.
PHOTO BY LARRY WEILL

"There were some large metal augers and other excavating tools located out in front, so I decided to replace them with something more entertaining," said Huta. "I completed the 'Gone Fishing' carving in 2004 or 2005, and it's just one of many that I've carved over the years. I've also done a bullfrog, a horse, a giraffe, and more."

Huta has many more talents that have kept him busy over the years. He also served as a certified public account (CPA) for quite a while and did tax returns as a side business in addition to his academic and artistic endeavors.

When asked if he has finished with his carving and sculpting hobby, the ambitious retiree says no. Born in 1941, he shows no sign of slowing down. "My latest carving was of a Minnesota Viking, for my grandchild who is a fan." As of the writing of this story, Huta's grandchildren ranged in age from 21 down to 12.

When asked about the "Private" sign on the "Gone Fishing" street sign, Huta notes that it was added by the town of Piseco. "I actually wanted them to call it 'Huta Way,' but that never happened."

Huta notes that all are welcome to stop and photograph his creative sculptures, as he enjoys providing the landmarks for the public to view. However, please respect that the camp itself is private property and is not open to the public. The "Gone Fishing" sign is on the left side of Route 8 as you approach the town of Piseco. The sculptures can be spotted on the side of the road.

HOMESTEAD OF JULIA PRESTON, EARLY FEMALE GUIDE

The aging log cabin that sits at 408 Old Piseco Road in the town of Piseco wouldn't attract much attention if not for the NY State historical marker sign that sits out front. The sign states that Julia Preston (who built the cabin) was one of the first female guides licensed in New York, and that she "worked in the North Woods in the early 1900s."

Julia Preston was a small, almost diminutive woman. However, in her personal and professional life, she was a veritable giant. Born in 1896, she lived much of her life in the outdoors, becoming a professional guide in the days when that field was completely male dominated. She worked the area around Piseco Lake and NY Route 10 and became known for her keen ability to lead clients to big game.

Log cabin home of Julia Preston, early Adirondack guide, in Piseco.
Photo by Larry Weill

The log cabin, situated back from the road, stands as a testament to her dogged determination to overcome obstacles. Although she did have help putting up the dwelling (her brother and uncle supposedly both aided in the construction), her husband (Charles Preston) was fighting in World War II during this period. Her four-foot-ten frame did not deter her from providing much of the muscle needed to raise the log cabin.

Julia was well known for other activities besides her guiding. Stories abound about her accuracy with her trusty Winchester rifle, which she not only used in the woods but also carried under her seat while working as a school bus driver in her community. According to her granddaughter,

Julia Preston (middle), early Adirondack guide.

PHOTO PROVIDED COURTESY OF THE PRESTON FAMILY

Kathy Hawkins, she found herself in trouble with the local authorities on more than one occasion for stopping the bus (a station wagon) to take down a passing deer.

Another story related by Kathy Hawkins involved a local game warden named Homer, who was also a friend of hers. Homer received a great many commendations upon his retirement, and he credited Preston with "teaching me everything I know about how to violate the game laws."

Historic marker outside the log cabin of Julia Preston, Adirondack guide.

PHOTO BY LARRY WEILL

Preston was also well known for collecting funds for various charities, including the Heart Fund, Cancer Foundation, and various tuberculosis associations. Hawkins said that despite her tough exterior and prowess with her Winchester, she also knitted, crocheted, and embroidered a variety of socks, scarves, and other garments, often to donate to those same charities.

Julia Preston lived in this house until the closing days of her life, when she suffered from dementia and strokes. She passed away in October 1969 at the age of 72. Her husband never lived in the house after she died, himself suffering from emphysema.

Today, the house is inhabited by Preston's granddaughter, who is proud of the heritage left behind by her historic grandparents. The house is privately owned and is not open to the public. The cabin can be easily viewed from the road; however, respect for their privacy is greatly appreciated.

OLD RILEY PUB IN PISECO

The Adirondacks aren't known for having a proliferation of businesses spread across their massive expanse. However, one enterprise that has flourished is the number and variety of pubs and barrooms. Dating back to the early days of the lumberjack bars, where the early woodsmen quenched their thirst after emerging from the forests, literally hundreds of drinking establishments have come and gone inside the Blue Line.

One of the few remaining pubs from the nineteenth century still standing is the Old Riley Pub, which can be found next to the Piseco Historical Society at 155 Old Piseco Road in the town of Piseco. Established sometime in the 1880s, it was originally located about 200 feet down the road from its current position.

Old Riley Pub in Piseco in 2019.

Photo by Larry Weill

"This was a pub that was built to serve the tannery workers and lumbermen," said Fred Adcock, who along with his wife Cindy runs the Piseco Historical Society. "It was called the Riley Pub because it was operated by Hugh Riley, whose name has forever been associated with the business."

"The fact that the building itself is still standing is nothing short of a miracle," said Adcock. "At one time, there were 12 bars between Piseco and the Lake Pleasant town line. However, all the others either burned down, or were collapsed beneath heavy winter snows. Simply put, this is the last one standing."

The structure might have been demolished, but it was saved by Gladys "Molly" Blackwell, who tried to donate the building to the Adirondack Museum in 1959. The museum turned down the offer, however, as it could not afford the cost of moving the building to Blue Mountain Lake. So it remained on Old Piseco Road, where it has been lovingly cared for by the Historical Society.

"The building housing the pub is open to the public, but only during limited times," said Adcock. Specifically, visitors can tour the building on weekends during the months of July and August. Approximately 120 visitors per year stop by the pub to check out its wealth of historical contents.

Front room of the Old Riley Pub.
Photo by Larry Weill

"We've got a lot of good stuff inside for the public to see, including many antiques that were representative of the area and era that was Piseco," said Adcock. "But these items were actually added later, and were not original items found in the pub." These include a canoe, various bottles, dining pieces, a boat anchor, and even an old ball and chain from the Auburn State Prison.

Patrons of the bar also included many of the local teamsters, plus other locals who made their living in the woods, including gum pickers such as Tim Crowley.

Stop on by the Riley Pub if you are in the area around Piseco. But the bar is no longer open for business, so your beer will have to come from someplace else.

HOW DID THAT TREE GET INSIDE HOSS'S STORE?

Face it: Trees are commonplace commodities in the Adirondack Park, so most of us don't bother giving them any more than a passing glance. But most of the time, trees are something you'd expect to see growing *outside* a house or store rather than inside, and this is where the one at Hoss's Country Corner Store is different.

Tree growing through the roof of Hoss's Country Corner Store in Long Lake.
PHOTO BY LARRY WEILL

58

Hoss's store is a bit unique anyway, a local landmark that is recognized and loved by just about anyone who has ever traveled through the Adirondacks. Situated at the crossroads in the middle of the small town of Long Lake, it is well known for selling just about anything related to the park. Whether customers are looking to refresh their fishing tackle boxes, pick up a locally themed sweatshirt, browse the extensive book section, or acquire an "Adirondacky" Christmas ornament, Hoss's carries it all. The longtime owners, John and Lorrie Hosley, have built a business that is hard to drive by without wanting to stop in for a peek.

From the front of the store, unless you look carefully, you don't notice that the tree protrudes through the peaked roof on the left side. Your

Tree growing through the first floor of Hoss's Country Corner Store.
Photo by Larry Weill

eye just makes the assumption that it must be growing behind the business, which is not the case. Even when you're inside, walking past the barbecue mitts and sunglasses on the first floor, the tree trunk doesn't stand out as being real. After all, lots of places utilize decorative tree trunks, posts and beams, etc., to lend the décor a more rustic appearance, right? Except in this case, it's genuine. The tree is definitely real.

The presence of the tree inside the store has a fascinating backstory, as it began its life outside of the original building. "The part of the store that is on the left side of the entrance was once a completely separate building," said Lorrie Hosley, one of the store owners. "When we bought the store (which used to be Freeman's Store) back in 1972, that other structure sat in back of the original store, and was turned sideways to its current position. That was back in the days when this place sold a lot of hardware and work equipment, and that back building was used mainly for storage."

"In 1988, when we decided to add the back building to the main part of the store, we realized we had an issue. John (owner) is an absolute wizard when it comes to moving buildings. But there was a pine tree standing in the way, and in these parts, we don't like getting rid of trees. So we moved the other building up,

Hoss's Country Corner Store, circa 1988, with young tree growing in front of left side of building.

but left a gap, and then built an extension between the two structures (including roof and floor) to enclose the tree."

It was quite a process, and the Hosleys consulted with forestry professors at the University of Syracuse for advice on how to keep the tree alive throughout the process.

The tree has continued to thrive and grow throughout the years, which has prompted the Hosleys to make further adjustments to the floor and roof to accommodate its growth. The effort has been worth it to the store owners, who love watching visitors marvel at the tree in the middle of the store.

Hoss's is located at 1142 Main Street, Long Lake, New York. The phone number for the store is 518-624-2481, and store hours are Monday through Friday 9 a.m.–5 p.m., Saturday 9 a.m.–6 p.m., and Sunday 9 a.m.–4 p.m.

Sadly, Lorrie Hosley has passed away since this section was written. Her family continues to operate the store in Long Lake.

RUINS OF THE OLD PISECO TANNERY

Many of the old ruins that were early Adirondack businesses are just that: old ruins. They are buried in thick woods or covered by vines and saplings that quickly obscure the past. The old saying that "nature reclaims its own very quickly" can be verified at any of these historical sites.

Stone foundation, part of the surviving ruins of the Old Piseco Tannery.
PHOTO BY LARRY WEILL

One of these crumbling remains can be observed in the woods about 150 feet back from the verge of Old Piseco Road in Piseco. The moss-covered boulders that form the walls run for hundreds of feet into the forest and represent all that is left of the Old Piseco Tannery.

It's no wonder that little else remains of this once-teeming complex. It was last used as a place of employment around 1900, which means that it has been permitted to "go wild" for more than 120 years. All of the foundations are visible above the leaf-covered soil, but the rest has been lost to the ravages of time and the rugged Adirondack climate.

"The building was probably erected around 1850, although it may have been a different business before it was a tannery," said Fred Adcock of the Piseco Historical Society. "It went by a variety of names, including the Old Piseco Tannery, the Silver Lake Tannery, and the Old Rudeston Tannery. It stayed in business as a tannery from the 1860s until right around 1900, when it closed down due to the reduced supply of local hemlock bark, which was used to process the leather hides in the tanning process. They were also fighting the newly developed synthetic chemicals which were revolutionizing the industry."

Remains of a well or vat hole at the Old Piseco Tannery.
Photo by Larry Weill

While the stone foundations are easy to see, the actual entrance into the old tannery complex is marked only by a ribbon that is tied to a tree, about 150 yards from the Piseco Historical Society building. Once you're in the woods, however, the foundation walls are easy to spot and run for quite some distance along the forest floor.

"The buildings were quite sizable," said Adcock, who led the author on a guided tour of the ruins. "The main vat house building was over 250 feet long and 120 feet wide, and was sided by an auxiliary building that was about half that size. And the entire area within those foundations is filled with the scattered remains of rusted equipment and debris. Some of it is unsafe to touch, which is why we encourage any visitors to stay a safe distance from these spots."

Although the site is not generally open for touring at this time (and many would have difficulty in locating the unmarked remains), the state has plans to change all that within the coming years. There are plans to designate it as a state historic site and construct an interpretive historical trail that will lead around the entire perimeter. Once this is completed, a marker and signboard will be placed on Old Piseco Road to mark the location for the public. As of this writing, visitation is not recommended.

HORROR IN THE WOODS: THE ROBERT GARROW SAGA

Many people experience a fear of being alone in the woods. Whether they are afraid of wild animals, or perhaps just the unknown, it is one of the reasons so many people carry a weapon with them on their forays into the depths of the forest.

In the spring and summer of 1973, this fear was most certainly justified. Robert Garrow, a deranged serial killer who preyed on victims across Upstate New York, was loose and hiding in the wooded areas of the Adirondack State Park. An experienced woodsman with advanced survival skills, he was known to travel over long distances, always evading the state, county, and local law authorities by his stealth and experience in the woods.

Although his trial took place in 1974, a juror recalled the details of the case in 2019. John Simons, of Piseco, New York, was part of the entire ordeal, seeing it from the close-up vantage point of the juror's box.

"Being a juror was the last thing in the world I expected," said Simons during an interview with the author. "I was literally walking along the road, heading home when the Sheriff drove up and handed me a subpoena to appear for jury

Robert Garrow, fugitive from the law, circa 1973.

selection. It was quite a surprise, but because I was a teacher at the time, I felt it was my civic duty to participate."

Even when Simons was called for his interview, he still didn't expect to be selected. "I knew a couple of the witnesses, and I knew the District Attorney, so I thought I'd be removed from consideration. But since so many of the jurors were senior citizens, the judge wanted 12 jurors and four alternates, not two alternates as was common at the time. I became the last juror seated, resulting in a full jury."

The trial was held in the Hamilton County Courthouse, which still stands at 102 County View Drive, Lake Pleasant, New York. It lasted for more than seven weeks (including the jury selection), and Simons remembered large parts of the proceedings. He was still quite young (age 29) during the trial in June 1974, and he believed he may have been the last surviving member of that jury.

"I still think of it every time I drive past that building," said Simons. "We heard some testimony that was pretty gruesome . . . pretty tough stuff to forget."

Garrow escaped from prison on more than one occasion, the final time from Fishkill Correctional Facility on September 8, 1978. He avoided capture for a few days but was fatally shot while exchanging gunfire with a number of corrections officers outside the prison. He was 42 years old at the time of his death.

Courthouse in Lake Pleasant, site of the Robert Garrow murder trial.
PHOTO BY LARRY WEILL

Although many suspect there were other victims who were never successfully linked to Garrow, he did confess to several killings in the Adirondacks, including in Hamilton County. Some of those sites can still be accessed today, although the rerouting of several roads and the revegetation of some campsites have hidden them from view. Nevertheless, this is one episode of Adirondack folklore that will always be remembered with horror around the campfire.

IN THE SERVICE OF HIS COUNTRY: MALCOLM L. BLUE MEMORIAL

It's not the kind of thing you expect to find in the middle of the woods, especially along a trail that has been aptly dubbed Cathedral Pines, in recognition of the stand of majestic conifers that tower over the forest like an army of giants. However, the stone casing that enshrines the memorial plaque is there, standing in dignified solitude for all to see and honor.

2nd Lieutenant Malcolm Blue, a member of the Eighth Air Force during World War II, was part of a 10-man crew onboard a Liberator bomber. That aircraft was shot down in action over France in the area of the Normandy beach-

Memorial to 2nd Lieutenant Malcolm L. Blue, Eighth Air Force.
PHOTO BY LARRY WEILL

2nd Lieutenant Malcolm L. Blue.

head invasion site, on June 2, 1944. It was Lt. Blue's very first mission flying over France. Of the crew, three were taken prisoner and two others (including Blue) were killed. The only account of Blue's death states that he suffered a fractured skull along with multiple other injuries.

Shortly after the war, the people of Poland, New York (Blue's hometown), had a plaque prepared honoring their hometown hero's service to his country. The plaque and the memorial site were dedicated in a ceremony presided over by Governor Thomas Dewey, accompanied by several other state officials and family members. The plaque is mounted inside the short loop trail through the Cathedral Pines in Inlet, New York.

At the time of the dedication, the plaque was affixed to an ancient white pine tree that forest rangers estimated to be 600 years old. The plaque was later moved to a stone memorial (pictured previously), which still stands today.

To find this plaque, follow NY Route 28 north of Inlet for about 3 miles. A small DEC trail sign is visible on the left side of the road. Parking is limited, but is available for a small number of cars on either side of the road. If you only wish to hike in to the memorial, follow the loop trail that branches off to the left. The memorial stone is about 200 feet down the trail. But the rest of the short loop is also worth seeing for the beautiful trees overhead.

Trailhead marker for Cathedral Pines, on NY Route 28.

THE MYSTERIOUS ORIGINS OF KUNJAMUK CAVE

Caves are kind of funny things. They can run the gamut of size, depth, and geological composition. To some folks, a "cave" invokes the image of a massive underground network of tunnel-like routes that are almost endless. Adorned with stalactites and stalagmites, they offer an unparalleled opportunity for spelunkers to explore and for novices to become lost.

However, Kunjamuk Cave, located in the village of Speculator, is different from these. It is officially listed as a cave, even though it was quite possibly excavated by humans. But no one knows who created it, or how, when, or why. It is a complete mystery that has withstood the investigations of the past century and then some.

By any standards, the cave is tiny, measuring a mere 15 feet in length. It is wide enough to permit two people to walk side by side, and with enough overhead clearance to allow even the tallest individual to remain upright.

Perhaps one of the most noticeable features of the cave is the presence of a hole overhead that leads through to the ground above. Those who believe the cave was man-made suggest that this hole was created to allow campfire smoke to vent to the outside rather than filling the cave with unbreathable air.

Entrance to Kunjamuk Cave outside Speculator.
PHOTO BY LARRY WEILL

67

Another interesting anecdote is that the cave was used as a stopover place for the famous local woodsman Adirondack French Louie on his way to or from his many camps in the West Canada Lakes area. (Louie lived in these woods from the 1870s until his death in 1915.) This is mainly a theory, as there is no existing proof other than the folklore of the region. But Louie knew the woods better than anyone back in his time, so the stories may be entirely true.

The author, during his visit to the cave, spent some time trying to identify any signs of excavation activity, without success. Without the inspection of an expert cave geologist (or speleologist), this mystery will probably remain unsolved.

To find Kunjamuk Cave, drive to "four corners" in Speculator, where NY Routes 30 and 8 intersect. Head north on Route 30 and turn right onto Elm Lake Road. At about 2 miles the road passes through a gate and then becomes rough and uneven. Keep to the right when the road forks, and follow Cave Hill Road (and other signs) until you arrive at the final roadside marker. When you pass over a fairly new wooden bridge, you'll know you are on the correct path. There is a place to park a few cars within a hundred yards of the cave marker, and the

Road signs and information displays on the local forest and wildlife near Kunjamuk Cave.

Photo by Larry Weill

cave itself is found within about 100 feet of the road. This area is never crowded, but please drive with care due to the rough roads and blind curves in the area.

IRISH ROAD BOWLING

If there's one thing that the residents of the Adirondacks know how to do, it's to have a good time in spite of the weather. Snow, sleet, ice, and freezing temperatures have never stopped them from getting out and enjoying themselves, especially if there is a good reason to throw a party. And Irish road bowling is as good a party as you'll find anywhere.

Anyone from outside the region will read that and ask, "what the heck is Irish road bowling?" The folks from the Indian Lake SnowWarriors Club will be happy to provide the answer. The 2023 version of the event was held the day after St. Patrick's Day, with a crowd of about 275 "bowlers" turning out to participate.

First of all, SnowWarriors is a snowmobile club that has been gathering together since 1967. It has about 300 members, who enjoy the winter months

Irish road bowling contestants dressed in costume for the event.
Photo by Larry Weill

69

just as much as the summer. The idea of the road bowling event originated about 10–15 years ago, and it has grown in size every year since.

One of the key players in this group activity is Ed LaScala, who originally came to the Adirondacks from his native New Jersey before purchasing a summer home in Indian Lake. He has since moved up to the Adirondacks as a year-round resident. Ed organizes the Irish road bowling event every year with a cadre of dedicated assistants. It has become a passion for this group, which is clearly evident as they go about their preparations on the morning of the contest.

To summarize, Irish road bowling involves teams of four individuals who take turns bowling (underhand) a heavy iron ball down a back road. There is a start line and a finish line, and the team that completes the route in the fewest rolls is pronounced the winner. The event is untimed, and each group starts its own rolls as soon as the previous group is safely "down range" of the next.

The iron balls, which are about 2 inches in diameter and weigh about 3 pounds each, resemble small cannon balls and roll remarkably well. (By the way, no one seems to know just where these spheres came from, but no one seems to care much either.)

One of the competitors, Lee Muran, spoke about the fun competition in which his team (the Couples Therapy team) had participated for the past five

Irish road bowler throwing the first ball at the starting line.
PHOTO BY LARRY WEILL

years. Muran is from the Corning area, and members of his team travel from Indian Lake, Syracuse, Pennsylvania, and beyond. "A lot of these folks came from a hunting club on the Cedar River Road that was established in the 1920s," he said. "Wearing the costumes is fun for everyone. I'm always easy to find; I'm the only one here who wears a kilt!"

When asked why he enjoys the competition so much every year, Muran quickly points to "the friendships, the camaraderie, and enjoying St. Patrick's Day to its fullest."

The Indian Lake road bowling competition has been conducted every year, despite some recent issues. The COVID pandemic put a damper on the 2020 version of the event, and a blizzard threatened to make things difficult in 2022. However, the organizing committee and the participants have refused to allow adversity to block their fun, and "the show has gone on" without interruption.

Heavy iron ball (approx. 3 pounds) used for Irish road bowling.
PHOTO BY LARRY WEILL

Ed LaScala said that the event has been moved among various roads in Indian Lake each year, just to keep things interesting. The town cooperates by closing the road to maintain the safety of the participants. The 2023 competition was held on the Chain of Lakes Road, with the length of the course measuring out at about 0.8 mile. Teams entered with creative names such as the Hot Mommas, the Lucky Charmers, and the Jello Shooters. Teams can compete as all-men, all-women, or mixed, with medals presented to the winners in each division.

Even though only one team from each division is declared a "winner," everyone there appears to enjoy the friendly competition to the hilt. The costumes, and fun, the food, and the drink (yes, there are alcoholic beverages present) all contribute to the festivities, and everyone has a great time. If you wish to become involved, you can do a search on "Indian Lake" and "Irish road bowling" to check out this event. To read more about this unusual winter pastime, visit https://www.adirondack.net/event/irish-road-bowling-141612. You don't even need to wear a kilt.

CARDBOARD SLED RACING

As if rolling an iron ball down a back road in the middle of winter isn't enough, here's another idea: Build yourself a jazzy sled out of nothing but cardboard and duct tape, then race your fellow competitors to the bottom of the hill. That's the idea behind Indian Lake's annual Cardboard Sled Race, and it's a real hoot for everyone involved.

The race has been going on for many years, said Christine Pouch, the events coordinator for the town of Indian Lake.

"I moved to the town about 18 years ago, and it had been going on for some time already," said Pouch. "I know they hold them in Long Lake and in Speculator as well, so they're very popular up here."

Competitors preparing for the big slide down the hill at Indian Lake.
Photo provided courtesy of Christine Pouch.

The Cardboard Sled Race is a popular event that is well attended every year. "We often have at least 30–50 competitors going down the hill," said Pouch. "There are three age categories: children under age 7, then 8 to 15, and then kids 16 and over. And that's one difference between our race versus the other towns; in Indian Lake, it's basically a race for the children rather than the grown-ups."

Like most contests, the Cardboard Sled Race has rules that must be followed by all contestants. First and foremost, all sleds must be constructed of nothing but cardboard and tape. There is some leeway provided in the kinds of tape and cardboard, so ingenuity is rewarded. For example, some contestants use duct tape while others use plastic shipping tape. "The runners are important," said Pouch, "because they have to be slippery in order to slide with as little friction as possible."

There are other rules that must also be followed by the riders. For example, the riders must be in the sled the entire ride from the top of the hill to the bottom. So if a contestant falls out of the sled, or steps out to push, they are disqualified.

"We also have some fun prizes as well," said Pouch. "We even give a prize for the most spectacular 'wipe-out' going down the hill. And prizes for the best sled design, and lots more. It's not entirely about speed. We make sure that everyone walks away with some prize. The kids really love it."

What a concept! The windmill sled on its way down the track.

The race is held every year (weather permitting) during Snocade, which is Indian Lake's winter festival. It's usually right around President's Day (in February), although it varies from year to year. The location is at the town's "ski hutch" on NY Route 30 near Big Brook Road. "There used to be an actual ski hill there, but it was discontinued due to lack of use. But there is still a large community center located there with a skating rink and a winter sports complex. The Cardboard Sled Race is held on the 2nd slope of the old ski hill."

The Cardboard Sled Race is open to everyone, whether local or from out of town. For more informtion, visit Indian Lake's website at https://indian lakeadk.com/.

TWO-FOR-ONE DEAL IN RAQUETTE LAKE

Nowhere else in this book will you see two such major and interesting attractions colocated at one place. In the following pages you will read about two very different modes of transportation (boat and caboose) that are, indeed, very closely related.

The photograph in the next entry shows the End-of-the-Line Caboose Gift Shop in the snow next to the *W. W. Durant* dinner boat, which is pulled out of the water once a decade for hull inspection by the state. They are both owned by the Raquette Lake Navigation Company.

Both of these unique and popular attractions were the inspirations of Dean and Donna Pohl, a husband-and-wife team whose visionary foresight has resulted in the "popularization" of Raquette Lake as a tourist destination.

The stories behind these two attractions are told over the next few pages.

END-OF-THE-LINE CABOOSE GIFT SHOP

Caboose train cars are seldom seen in the modern world, even by those who frequent train yards and railway routes. That's because the caboose car was formally retired in 1984, a victim of smaller train crews and electronic advancements. However, if you want to not only visit a caboose but also go inside for some great Adirondack souvenir shopping, the place to go is the dock on the southwest side of Raquette Lake.

The bright red caboose that sits across from the boat dock is as eye-catching as it is seemingly out of place. After all, there is no train (or train tracks) in the area, so tourists are left to wonder how it got there.

End-of-the-Line Caboose Gift Shop in Raquette Lake.
PHOTO BY LARRY WEILL

The caboose was originally purchased many years ago by Dean and Donna Pohl from a "caboose graveyard" in Reading, Pennsylvania. From there, the train car was transported on its own wheels to Utica, New York, where it was loaded onto a flatbed truck for the 75-mile ride to Raquette Lake. "The wheels were loaded onto a separate truck," recalled Donna. "They weren't reunited until they arrived up here at the lake."

Once in Raquette Lake, the caboose sat empty as a conversation piece for over a decade. "Dean loved trains," said Donna of her late husband. (Unfortunately, Dean passed away in May 2023.) "He loved them so much that he once paid money just to sit in the engineer's seat on a train in New Hampshire or Connecticut. He just loved the experience."

Finally, one winter day the couple was talking about how the caboose could be an income producer instead of just a conversation piece. They decided that the caboose would make a great gift shop. Dean built the cupola, then added a small extension to the back of the car to include enough space for the clerk and a desk. Other finishing touches were added, and the rest is history.

Once you enter the train car and look around, you will be amazed at just how much merchandise is on display. The shop features jewelry, clothing, books, drink mixes and snacks, room decorations, and lots more.

"In addition to having a very large stock, we're also proud to say that at least 95 percent of our merchandise is made in the USA," said Sydney Pohl, who manages the shop. "We have great merchandise at competitive prices, and almost all of it is manufactured right here at home. We're very proud of that fact."

Sydney is married to Jim Pohl, who serves as the celebrated chef on the *W. W. Durant* dinner boat, which docks next to the gift shop. It's a family affair of great people who have helped make the town of Raquette Lake a popular tourist destination. The gift shop is on Church Road, Raquette Lake, New York. There is no street number; it is the only thing on that street aside from the boat pier.

Sydney Pohl, manager of the End-of-the-Line Caboose Gift Shop, greets visitors as they enter.

PHOTO BY LARRY WEILL

W. W. DURANT DINNER BOAT

Sitting across from the caboose gift shop is the other half of the Raquette Lake Navigation Company's major attractions: the *W. W. Durant* dinner boat. This craft was another brainchild of Dean and Donna Pohl. The hull was built in two halves in Escanaba, MI, which were then shipped from Michigan on two flatbed trucks.

"Once it arrived, dad had a certified welder weld the two hull halves together. Dad then did all the welding from the waterline up, and all the carpentry," said Rachel Pohl, daughter of the entrepreneur. "He was a master carpenter, among other things. He built the entire boat with the help of three employees."

The construction took two and a half winters to complete. It is a large vessel, so there was a lot of work to tackle. "The construction was mainly

The *W. W. Durant* dinner boat sitting dockside in Raquette Lake.
<small>PHOTO PROVIDED COURTESY OF RACHEL POHL</small>

accomplished in the winter, since Dean was busy earning a living from April through November as a general contractor and builder," said Rachel. "Many days the crew would have to shovel snow off the decks for the first two hours before they could even start pounding nails."

The completed boat was launched on May 29, 1991. Its maiden voyage was one month later, on June 29. The boat is 60 feet long and weighs 57 tons.

Rachel likes to point out that all four of the siblings (children of Dean and Donna) worked on the boat at one time or another. Of the four, only Rachel and her brother Jim continue to work every season. The other two children made other career choices. Rachel has held numerous positions on the boat and now serves as its captain on many of the tours. Jim is the chef, preparing memorable meals in the galley.

Inside the dining room of the *W. W. Durant*.
Photo provided courtesy of Rachel Pohl

"On many dinner boats, the tour itself is the main attraction, and the meal is sort of an afterthought. But on our boat, Jim is a CIA (Culinary Institute of America)-trained chef. The dinners served onboard can compete with any fine dining experience in any city. We are very proud of the quality of our food."

Speaking with Rachel, one can truly feel the pride she has in the boat and her family's involvement in the community. "This is our 32nd season on the boat; I turned 13 on its maiden voyage. You might say my entire life has been dedicated to it."

The dinner tour is three hours long and is fully narrated. The captain's narration is very important to the family because Dean's voice is recorded on the soundtrack. It really is a family affair.

The boat holds 100 passengers for its sightseeing tour, but fewer (66) for the dinner cruise, and even fewer (56) for lunch. The boat can also be chartered by individuals or groups for special events, including weddings and other family or corporate affairs.

Rachel says that the dinner cruises can sometimes book up several weeks in advance, while at other times you can still get a reservation the same day. It's best to call at least a week in advance to ensure a spot onboard.

Rachel Pohl posing on the bow of the *W. W. Durant*.
PHOTO BY LARRY WEILL

Raquette Lake Navigation Company is located at 224 Main Street, Raquette Lake, New York. You can reach the company by phone at 315-354-5532. For information on cruises, visit www.raquettelakenavigation.com/cruises.

"THE BOOB" ROCK AND SWIM HOLE

Sometimes a natural attraction doesn't require a formal name. Sometimes something in nature resembles an object so accurately that it just names itself. People adopt the name, which is then passed down from generation to generation and becomes part of the folklore of the area.

Such a spot exists on the southern end of Long Lake. There, a rock outcropping with a rounded, downward slope has appropriately been named "The Boob" rock swim hole. This is due to the pronounced resemblance of the rock to, well, the obvious.

"The Boob" is not maintained or operated by the town of Long Lake. In fact, it is not even accessible by land. To visit the place, you must travel by boat and then gain access via a route from the foot of the rock formation. The short-

"The Boob" rock, viewed from across Long Lake at Long View Lodge.
PHOTO BY LARRY WEILL

est way to get there is to drive your car *with your own boat* to Long View Lodge, which is located on the southeast side of Long Lake about a half-mile southwest of Hoss's store. From the piers in front of the Long View Lodge you can see Boob Rock on the opposite shore (looking to the left a bit, which is west). You will find a trail on the shoreline to the right of the rocks.

While investigating this popular site, I spoke with a local resident outside of the Long View Lodge who mentioned that the swim hole had been in use for many years. "I can tell you for a fact that at least four generations of my own family have jumped from that rock," he said. "It may go back even farther, but I know that much for sure."

Ms. Hallie Bond, town historian of Long Lake, described jumping off "The Boob" as a high school rite of passage. "I did it once, a very long time ago," she recalled. "But one thing I remember is that you have to leap from the right location, and you have to get a running jump at it. If you don't jump out far enough from the cliff, you can hit the rock wall on the way down."

Bond also recalled some of the folklore attached to "The Boob." "If you look closely enough at the rocks you can see a spot where they are stained a

Long View Lodge on Deerland Road in Long Lake. "The Boob" can be viewed from the boat dock behind the property.

<small>PHOTO BY LARRY WEILL</small>

reddish color. According to the story, a logger was once up there with a team of horses. The horses supposedly got startled by a bear and sprinted to the edge of the rock ledge. Unable to stop, they tumbled over the drop-off and skinned their knees on the way down to the water."

It is also important to note that jumping from "The Boob" may be hazardous, as there is shallow water below. "I know of at least one young man who tried to jump off there and injured himself very badly," said Bond. "You have to know where to jump and where to land. That is really important."

If you decide to visit "The Boob," it is best to go with someone who is familiar with the area and can provide guidance as to the safest place to leap. The town does not supervise this site or provide a lifeguard.

ATTRACTIONS OF FRANKLIN COUNTY

REMNANTS OF THE COLD WAR IN THE ADIRONDACKS

Even many Adirondack enthusiasts who have traveled the length of the park have never set foot in Vermontville, a small community located in Franklin County settled in the late 1840s. The scene is overwhelmingly rural, even by Adirondack standards, and "watch out for moose" signs appear frequently alongside the roads and byways.

Because of this seemingly pastoral background, it is almost impossible to conceive of the sinister installation that is present just over the hillside. There, hidden on an unmarked hilltop site that is not open to the public, rests one of the original Atlas ICBM missile silos left over from the Cold War.

Sign on the front of the Atlas Hoofed It Farm in Vermontville.

Most tourists passing through the area would not guess that the Adirondack Park was selected by our government as an ideal location for 12 of these massive weapons. Construction of the actual silos was started between 1956 and 1960, depending on which site is discussed.

The site is now on the property owned by Dan and Sara Burke, a couple of well-educated and energetic Adirondackers who met while attending Paul Smith's College many years ago. Dan is an expert carpenter who is a renowned producer of fancy Adirondack-style structures, furniture, and almost anything else made of wood. He is unique in that he does his own logging, using horses to sled the logs out of the woods to produce his works. Sara earned her degree in environmental chemistry before migrating into the field of medicine and health care, where she now serves as an RN. They both work double duty in their chosen fields while raising their two children and tending to chores on their hilltop farm.

"As you can see, we have a lot of almost everything, from chickens and hogs to horses and cows. But it's a great place to be and we both love taking care of the animals," said Sara.

Cows on hillside near the Atlas missile silo. Note the raised helicopter pad on the right rear side of the photo.

Photo by Larry Weill

Because the site is located on private property, it is completely unmarked and inconspicuous. The dirt road leading up the hill looks like any other of a thousand similar roads in the area, although it was once completely fenced off with barbed wire and other protective impediments. As Sara mentioned, "The ground is loaded with metals that are remnants from the installation. We're constantly finding bits and pieces as they work their way to the surface."

Entrance to the underground bunker and missile control center.
PHOTO BY LARRY WEILL

Much of the original site is now impossible to view, as the actual silo is flooded to within 40 feet of the surface. Dan made an adventurous excursion through the upper blast doors, which involved rappelling onto a raft that had been floated onto the water's surface. It was a dark and dangerous activity, compounded by the fact that there are still countless rounds of live ammunition residing inside the silo.

One aspect of the Burkes' existence in this unique setting is their overall philosophy of making something good out of what was undeniably a scary scene. Instead of thinking of the site as the home of an intercontinental ballistic missile, they have been raising livestock and putting the ground to good use.

"We even used the underground bunker space

Stairs leading down into the missile control center.
PHOTO BY LARRY WEILL

that had served as the missile crew's living quarters as an aging room for a local brewery," said Dan Burke. "I was friends with one of the brew masters at the Big Slide Brewery. They asked us if they could use our underground bunker to age their Russian Imperial Stout beer, which sat in that room at 55 degrees for a full year. And what better use of a facility that was built for a possible nuclear war with Russia than to age the Russian-style beer? It seemed like a perfect fit!"

Thankfully, the missile that used to be housed in the silo has been gone for well over 50 years, and the space is now used for peaceful endeavors. Because this is now private property, the owners (as well as the author) request that you respect their privacy and avoid trespassing on or around their farm. But if you wish to purchase eggs, beef, pork, or their other wonderful farm products, you can call them at 518-891-9586, or visit https://www.facebook.com/pages/category/Farm/Atlas-Hoofed-It-Farm-209354502428900/.

ANIMALS OF THE ADIRONDACK CAROUSEL

There aren't a lot of ways to improve on a good, old-fashioned merry-go-round. But one idea would be to fill the ride with animals, fish, and birds that are native to the forests and streams of the Adirondack Park. And that is just what you'll find at the Adirondack Carousel in Saranac Lake.

Entrance to the pavilion containing the Adirondack Carousel in Saranac Lake.
Photo by Larry Weill

The carousel was originally the brainchild of local Saranac Lake artist and woodcarver Karen Loffler. She first conceived of the idea of a carousel that was not only crafted by hand from wood but also used a full slate of endemic animals, fish, and birds as riding seats. Starting in 1999, Loffler worked tirelessly on the concept for 10 years, enlisting the help of others in the community to raise funds and advance the cause.

Finally, after years of work, the town of Saranac Lake decided to donate land for the carousel inside the historic William Morris Park, and the project vaulted into overdrive. As the pavilion enclosing the ride was built (the ground breaking was in 2011), a national search for accomplished wood carvers was conducted, and those individuals were sent a list of animals to be installed on the new carousel. These artists then submitted their ideas and proposals for bringing these animals to life.

The animals on the ride share a number of unique characteristics, some of which may be hidden to the riders. All the animals are carved from basswood, which is a light, soft wood that is very stable and easy to carve. It is found across large portions of the eastern United States and is easy to dye or stain. For these reasons, it was a natural choice for the project.

Another item that is common across all the animal seats is a rather whimsical addition to the painted surfaces; a ladybug has been hidden somewhere on the exterior of each animal. You can look for the ladybug on your own seat, but please make it a priority to hang onto the ride.

A fox and a trout appear to vie for first place on the carousel platform.

Photo by Larry Weill

Of particular interest on this attraction is the superb artwork found on each and every animal. While there are 22 animal carvings that serve as riding seats, only 18 of them are actually mounted and in use at any given time. Others can be found standing in fixed positions around the outside of the carousel platform.

Also present are a series of beautiful paintings located above the ride platform. These works of art have all been created by local artists and represent scenes of nature or famous buildings and events in the Saranac area.

The carousel's director, Jennifer Hunt, takes great pride in the carousel and extends a warm welcome to everyone in the area to stop by. "It doesn't matter if you are four, or ninety-four," said Hunt during a recent tour of the facility. "It's just fun, and it's art, and it's a part of everything that is Saranac Lake and the Adirondacks."

The carousel pavilion is found at 2 Depot Street, with parking available on the street. Hours of operation vary greatly between seasons and over special holiday weekends, so check online for times during your visit. The website for the carousel is http://www.adirondackcarousel.org/, and the phone number is 518-891-9521. Rides are $2.50 each, although discounts are available for multiple ride packages.

WINTER CARNIVAL IN SARANAC LAKE

The Adirondack Park is well known for its pronounced variance in climate from summer to winter, and each season is popular for its own slate of sports, activities, and festivals. Perhaps no event is more popular or better attended than the Winter Carnival in Saranac Lake each January.

The ice palace, completely constructed and on display as part of the 2020 Winter Carnival in Saranac Lake.
PHOTO BY LARRY WEILL

The hardy residents who claim Franklin County as their home, along with those enthusiastic tourists who aren't afraid of the cold, look forward to this annual event in Saranac Lake. The carnival, which has been in "almost-continuous" operation since its inception in 1897, is one of the most popular celebrations inside the Adirondack Blue Line.

"This is the longest-running event of its type," said Colleen O'Neill, the public affairs officer on the organizing committee. "The Winter Carnival has been in operation every year with the exception of a couple years around some of our major wars."

O'Neill also mentioned that the carnival and ice palace is open 24 hours a day, 7 days a week. There is no admission price to enter the ice palace, which was first built in 1898.

While the ice palace is perhaps the best-known visible feature of the Winter Carnival, there are a cluster of other events taking place in and around the area. The carnival extends over a 10-day period at the end of January and into February and includes parties, dinner gatherings, seminars, athletic events, competitions, and demonstrations. These run the full gamut from "Royal Dinners" and musical productions to hockey games and ice sculpting contests.

Nighttime view of the illuminated ice palace.
PHOTO BY LARRY WEILL

"It's really difficult to estimate how many people attend the Winter Carnival every year," said O'Neill. "We don't charge admission, and some of the events draw thousands of spectators, such as the parade and the fireworks."

The ice palace itself is a community project each year and uses about 100 volunteers to cut the ice blocks from the lake and move them into position. It's a labor of love, with numerous skilled ice builders toiling alongside dozens of novice workers who are there solely to provide the strong backs required to complete the job.

Sometimes Mother Nature does not cooperate, and the lake does not freeze thick enough to permit the construction of the ice palace on the lake. In 2020, the lake was partially open, and the ice that was present could not be trusted to support the weight. However, the carnival goes on regardless of the weather, and the ice palace is built on the shoreline around the lake in warmer years.

The Winter Carnival in Saranac Lake is just one of many wintertime celebrations in the Adirondacks; check online for others if your schedule precludes attending this one in particular. If you are able to make it to Saranac Lake for Winter Carnival, you can check the schedule of events at https://www.saranac

Ice sculpture of the Olympic ski jump, created by the Women's Civic Chamber of Saranac Lake.
PHOTO BY LARRY WEILL

lakewintercarnival.com/schedule. If you would like to attend, it is highly recommended that you make hotel reservations well in advance, as the Adirondacks are heavily used in the winter months by skiers and other winter enthusiasts. (You can expect to pay a premium for your accommodations during these months.) Also remember to bring along extra layers of warm, noncotton clothing, hats, socks, and gloves, as temperatures can reach –40° F during the coldest winter months.

CURLING IN THE ADIRONDACKS

There is no doubt that the sport of curling gained a lot of publicity during the Winter Olympic games of 2018. Television viewers in the United States were fed a continuous diet of circular granite disks gliding down glistening tracks of ice, while uniformed sweepers conditioned the ice in front of each throw. However, not many visitors to the region around Lake Placid and Saranac Lake are aware that the area serves as a hotbed of activity for this little-understood sport.

"Curling has actually been around for a very long time," said Amber McKernan, a leading member of the Lake Placid Curling Club and recognized expert on all that is local curling. "The earliest known curling took place in Scotland and is documented with a curling stone etched with the date of 1511, and it has been developing as a sport ever since then."

Members of the Lake Placid Curling Club gathered at a club event in Saranac Lake.
PHOTO BY LARRY WEILL

Curling is not new to the Olympics. It was a full Olympic sport as early as 1928. The Lake Placid Curling Club was founded in 1981, but there were other groups in existence earlier than that. "It's moved around the area over the years," explained McKernan. "Our club had its origins in Lake Placid at the Olympic Ice Center, which was moved to Saranac Lake Civic Center in October 2013. There have also been other curling clubs in the Saranac Lake area in the past, including one that conducts its games on Moody Pond. But since they play the game outdoors, they have to clear off the ice each time before they began."

Curling is known for being a very friendly and social game, which is why so many of the local participants got into the sport in the first place. "It's completely social by its very nature," said Steve Urquhart, who serves as the current president of the Lake Placid Curling Club. "All four team members are involved in every shot; you can't do it alone. Not only do you need your 'Skip' (skipper) to direct the path of the stone, but your two sweepers can literally make or break each shot."

Curlers who actively play the sport also point out that the activity is much more demanding than it looks on television. It isn't just the action of throwing

Members of the Lake Placid Curling Club teaching newcomers the principles of the sport, on Saranac Lake during the Winter Carnival.
Photo by Larry Weill

the stone, which weighs about 42 pounds, plus or minus a couple pounds. The first and second positions on the team walk about 2 miles each match, up and down the "sheet" (a distance of 146 feet from one end to the other), which is supplemented by the action of frenetically sweeping the ice in advance of each stone. "Most first and second position team members burn as many calories each match as they would playing a full set of tennis," said McKernan. "It's a lot more strenuous and involved than it appears on TV."

The participants are also very friendly and encouraging to one another, and the losing team always congratulates the winners at the end of each match. "But that's okay, the winning team is expected to buy the drinks following the conclusion of the match," said McKernan. "They don't have to be alcoholic beverages, but they are very much part of the post-match ritual."

The Lake Placid Curling Club owns much of its own equipment, which is a good thing in a sport with such specialized gear. "A complete set of curling stones consists of 16 granite stones that can cost upward of $8,000. The granite comes from some very select locations off the coast of Scotland and Wales," explained McKernan. "The very best granite is mined off a single island in the Firth of Clyde in the Irish Sea. It's called Ailsa Craig, and it is special because its granite contains very little quartz, thus making its molecular bonds much stronger than usual."

Curling stones resting on the target, or "house," at Saranac Lake Civic Center.
PHOTO BY LARRY WEILL

The Lake Placid Curling Club has moved its games inside Saranac Lake Civic Center on Sunday afternoons from mid-October to the end of March. The sport is focused around the winter months, but indoor ice facilitates curling on a year-round basis. Anyone interested in stopping by to watch is welcome. The Lake Placid Curling Club's website is at http://lakeplacidcurling.com/. The club also has several trained instructors and coaches to teach new curlers how to play the game and improve their performance. Individuals interested in learning how to play can contact the league at lpcurling@gmail.com.

INSIDE THE CRAZY WORLD OF LOONS

Just about everyone has heard the expression "crazy as a loon." Yet most Americans have not met one of these aquatic waterfowl up close and personal. One exception to this rule is the hikers who traverse the trails around the lakes and waterways of the Adirondack wilderness.

Streetside view of the Adirondack Center for Loon Conservation in Saranac Lake, New York.
Photo by Larry Weill

"We are quite lucky in that we have an abundance of these magnificent birds inside the Adirondack Park," says Liz DeFonce, administrative assistant at the Adirondack Center for Loon Conservation in Saranac Lake. "It's truly a privilege being able to observe and study these birds as they exist in their natural habitat, right here in our own backyard."

The common loon, known scientifically as *Gavia immer*, has made its home in the Adirondacks for thousands of years. Those hikers who make it through to the inner sanctums of the Adirondack wilderness are familiar with the eerie repertoire of these waterfowl as their calls pierce the night. It is one of those things that makes a camping trip a truly Adirondack experience, even though their territorial boundaries far exceed the geographic confines of the park.

The director of the Adirondack Center for Loon Conservation is Dr. Nina Schoch, who became involved in 1998 through her desire to immerse herself in the study of ecological conservation. She originally worked on a three-year study with the Biodiversity Research Institute in Maine before expanding her work to a multiagency collaboration of five organizations, all focusing on the conservation and preservation of local endemic species. In 2016, she was encouraged to

Loon with newly hatched chick, on display inside the Adirondack Center for Loon Conservation.

Photo by Larry Weill

branch out on her own, which led to the establishment of the Adirondack Center for Loon Conservation in its current location in 2017. The center performs a variety of studies and annual monitoring on the local loon populations. "Loons are an excellent indicator species," said Schoch. "They live for 20–30 years, so annual changes in their bodies and the accumulated levels of toxins can be easily measured and compared to local environmental conditions."

Schoch described the annual collecting and testing of loons, which takes place for a one-week period each year. "We generally field-capture 10–20 birds each year, which are then tested using noninvasive techniques, including feather and blood samples. From these tests we can determine the accumulations of toxins in their bodies, along with possible consequences to the breeding populations in these lakes."

The Adirondack Center for Loon Conservation building is located at 15 Broadway in Saranac Lake, New York. It is open to the public daily from 10 a.m. to 5 p.m., except Tuesday, when it's open from 11 a.m. to 5 p.m. It is often confused with a store offering various souvenirs of loons and their habitats. Items available for purchase include loon T-shirts, mugs, jewelry, and artwork commemorating the waterfowl. However, the main objective of the staff (which

Skeletal structure of a loon, on display at the Adirondack Center for Loon Conservation.
Photo by Larry Weill

utilizes many volunteers to accomplish its work) is the study and preservation of the Common Loon.

For more information on the Adirondack Center for Loon Conservation, visit https://www.adkloon.org or call 518-354-8636. Visits are free, but donations are greatly appreciated.

ROBERT LOUIS STEVENSON HOUSE

The small white residence, or "cottage," on an elevated side street in Saranac Lake doesn't appear to be anything out of the ordinary in this aging Adirondack town. There are no statues on the lawn or ivy-covered brick walls to proclaim its status as a landmark of literary significance. In fact, only the sign and hours of operation billboard on the exterior of the white-shingled building advertise its noteworthiness as a historic dwelling.

Yet the small habitation served as the temporary home of Robert Louis Stevenson from October 3, 1887, until his departure on April 16, 1888. Stevenson, the author of such classics as *Treasure Island, The Master of Ballantrae,* and *The*

Side entrance to the Robert Louis Stevenson Memorial Cottage in Saranac Lake.
PHOTO BY LARRY WEILL

Strange Case of Dr. Jekyll and Mr. Hyde, never intended to stay in the Adirondacks or in New York State at all. He was en route to Colorado under the orders of his physician, who believed that the Colorado air would have a restorative effect on his respiratory illness. (He was believed to have suffered from tuberculosis at the time, although that has been disputed in the century since his death.) However, Stevenson, who had suffered a lifetime of chronic illness, became too afflicted to make the journey across the country and ended up settling in Saranac Lake for six months.

The earliest sections of the cottage were built in 1855, which include the part that is the modern-day museum. The remaining rooms were built between 1866 and 1887, the year of Stevenson's arrival. Even though the author's tenure in the house was

Portrait of Robert Louis Stevenson on the wall of the Memorial Cottage in Saranac Lake.

PHOTO BY LARRY WEILL

relatively brief, the local Robert Louis Stevenson Society has maintained this local landmark as a shrine to the famous tenant.

The residence is operated today as a museum, and the rooms are literally crammed with manuscripts, photographs, and furniture that was present when Stevenson was in residence. The curator of the museum is Mike Delahant, who represents the third generation of his family to be involved with the building.

"My grandfather, John F. Delahant Sr., came up from New Jersey in 1953 to visit, but broke his ankle and had to remain in the area," said Delahant. "The town of Saranac Lake was looking for a custodian for the museum, so they hired him, and he became the president of the Robert Louis Stevenson Society of America. When he passed in 1958, my father, John F. Delahant Jr., took over the position."

Mike Delahant moved to Saranac Lake in 1980, 22 years after the passing of his grandfather. Although he originally performed only groundskeeping duties around the museum, he has since become deeply committed to all aspects of the preservation of the museum and its collection. Delahant occupies the attached residence on the other side of the building, where he can keep an eye on the facility on a daily basis.

"It's been a labor of love," said Delahant, who has personally researched and written almost 100 articles and essays on various aspects of Robert Louis Stevenson's life and his time in Lake Placid. "At times, there have been repairs needed in the house that I've taken care of out of my own pocket. There really isn't much funding available through the town, so it's been up to me, along with whatever we receive in the form of donations."

The Robert Louis Stevenson Memorial Cottage is open daily except Monday from July 1 through September 15. Its hours of operation are 9:30 a.m.–noon and from 1:00–4:30 p.m. In the winter months, the curator will open it when requested in advance. He can be reached at the museum at 518-891-1462. For additional information, visit the website at http://robert-louis-stevenson.org/107-baker-cottage-saranac-lake/.

Small desk where Stevenson did much of his writing. He also wrote music at this desk and played it on a piano that used to stand next to it.
PHOTO BY LARRY WEILL

Sculpted bust of Stevenson, cast in Hawaii by British sculptor Alan Hutchinson. The bust is on display in the living room of the Memorial Cottage.
PHOTO BY LARRY WEILL

LAKE CLEAR LODGE & RETREAT

I must admit that, as the author of this book, I was originally drawn to this "attraction" solely because of its reputation as a 1920s speakeasy. It was one of many buildings and businesses in existence to help the rumrunners of the Prohibition Era avoid law enforcement authorities as they chased the illegal alcoholic spirits around the North Country. It was a romantic period in our country's history that still fascinates many citizens. Otherwise stated, speakeasies make for popular folklore.

View inside the back room of the main lodge at Lake Clear Lodge & Retreat.
Photo by Larry Weill

As I followed Cathy Hohmeyer around the main lodge in Lake Clear, I quickly discovered that this facility is so much more than just a speakeasy. It offers a HUGE variety of activities, food, and other events to please almost every variety of visitor.

Cathy, who runs the business side of Lake Clear Lodge & Retreat, mentions that the community is located relatively close to the Canadian border, which is the reason a number of the nearby buildings also had hidden cellars and subterranean rooms. Even if they did not serve alcohol, they could be used for hiding and storing these beverages until they could be moved on to their final destinations.

The back room of the lodge (and the stairwell to the downstairs speakeasy) is accessed through a door that is camouflaged to resemble a bookcase. There is a photograph mounted in the middle of that door that has a hidden viewing slit. Visitors to the speakeasy needed to state the password and be "approved" before they were allowed to enter.

Both Cathy and her husband Earnest have a long and involved history with this establishment. The building itself, which is one of the last great Adirondack lodges, was constructed in 1886. The builders and original owners were the Otis

Lower-level bar concealing the entrance to the wine cellar.
Photo by Larry Weill

family, who were Cathy's great-aunt and great-uncle. He served as the postmaster of Lake Clear, and some of the original postal furniture and equipment is still present in the lodge's front room.

Earnest's parents purchased the lodge in 1965, and Cathy worked there in 1974–1975. Earnest and Cathy bought the lodge in 1990, so their lives have been thoroughly entwined in the property for many decades.

The downstairs areas of the speakeasy have been ingeniously designed to hide the intent of the business, which was to serve illegal alcohol to Prohibition Era clientele. Everything about the lower level has been constructed to prevent the police from finding the liquor, from the hidden wine cellar to the bar itself (which is quickly converted into a library shelf). There are drink tables that invert into tea tables, as well as an alarm system that sounds off when a raid is about to take place. Earnest built the wine and beer cellar into a room that is concealed behind the bar, which is an incredibly clever use of disguise. It all just works.

Despite the obvious allure of the speakeasy, visitors to the Lake Clear Lodge & Retreat will find so much more in the same setting. One of the main attractions at this place is the fine dining, which is specifically tailored to represent the Adirondack region through various periods of its history. Cathy serves as the execu-

Wine cellar in the lower level of the speakeasy.
Photo by Larry Weill

tive chef (she also teaches cooking classes), and she enjoys leading her patrons through the "Five Eras of Adirondack Food." Visitors can dine in the speakeasy restaurant and are welcome to wear Prohibition Era clothing, although this is certainly not required.

The lodging rooms at Lake Clear Lodge have been built by Earnest. The rooms can hold about 50 people, and they offer a variety of different settings and décor. There is also a conference center on the premises that can handle about 100 people and is available to rent for meetings or retreats.

In addition to the lodging and themed dining, the lodge also offers horse-drawn sleigh rides (in winter) and carriage rides (in summer), which are available for a reasonable fee. Trails run through the lodge's property between the lodge and the lake, where gorgeous views of the sunset can be witnessed daily.

Bottles of Lake Clear "Gaggle Water" on display at the speakeasy bar.
Photo by Larry Weill

When Cathy is asked how Lake Clear Lodge & Retreat is different from other Adirondack lodge experiences, she is quick to point out that they enjoy providing experiences that "rejuvenate while having fun and interacting with nature."

The Lake Clear Lodge & Retreat is located at 6319 NY Route 30, Lake Clear, New York 12945. The lodge can be reached by phone at 518-891-1489, or visit www.LakeClearLodge.com.

GHOSTS & GUESTS OF HOTEL SARANAC

Hotel Saranac is not only one of the oldest and most distinguished hotels in the town of Saranac Lake, it is one of the largest buildings in the town as well. The hotel has gone through quite a few renovations and updates over the years in its attempt to remain modern and attractive to the Adirondack tourist crowd that flocks to the area every year.

Front view of Hotel Saranac in Saranac Lake.
PHOTO BY LARRY WEILL

While the hotel retains its reputation for providing clean and luxurious accommodations as well as attractive restaurants and shops, many people visit the premises because of its history of supernatural phenomena. Stories abound about its haunted background and cast of "visitors" from a different era. It makes for a fun and interesting sideline to a stay at the famous hotel.

"A lot of places with haunted reputations tend to shun the stories, afraid that people may stay away because of the ghost stories," says Braylin Jones, the hotel's front office manager. "But Hotel Saranac embraces our past and the stories that have grown throughout our history. It adds to the mystique of the place, and our guests are interested."

Photograph of original Saranac Lake High School. The school burned to the ground, and the hotel was built on top of the limestone foundations in 1927.

PUBLIC DOMAIN

Many of the hotel guests have reported seeing "the Professor," a scholarly looking fellow who appears in an old-fashioned top hat. Reportedly he was a teacher at the old school, and he has been sighted in the basement between the fitness center and the utility room. "Those rooms were built directly over the limestone ruins of the old school building, so that kind of makes sense," said Jones.

Another guest of the hotel supposedly had a cat with them when they passed away in their room. To this day, the cat still roams the hallways of the hotel and has been spotted by a number of the guests. Other supernatural events have been reported on the third and sixth floors.

To date, all of the incidents have been harmless, and no one has reported a spirit showing up in their room. But the sights and sounds have been observed by a great many people over the years, including both employees and hotel guests. So . . . who knows?

Fourth-floor hallway of Hotel Saranac, where a young girl has been heard singing on numerous occasions.
PHOTO BY LARRY WEILL

The hotel is located at 100 Main Street in Saranac Lake. The phone number is 518-891-6900, and the website is www.hotelsaranac.com. Accommodations are very reasonably priced and can be made online. The hotel also offers a variety of suites and premium suites to meet the specific needs of your stay. Any ghosts tagging along with you are permitted to stay for free.

SARANAC LABORATORY MUSEUM

Consumption. It's a word that doesn't mean much to people today. But in the 1800s, it represented the specter of a horrible disease that often resulted in death or severe incapacitation. It often struck from out of nowhere, causing the victim to suffer from severe coughing, difficulty breathing, weakness, weight loss, fever, and more. The disease can also spread to other parts of the body, and often needs to be treated with antibiotics to fully cure the patient.

In 1873, Dr. Edward Livingston Trudeau, a physician born in New York City and practicing on Long Island, contracted tuberculosis. Unfortunately there

Saranac Laboratory Museum, photographed from across
Church Street in Saranac Lake.
PHOTO BY LARRY WEILL

were no medicines available to cure it; Alexander Fleming didn't discover penicillin (the first antibiotic) until 1928. So Trudeau decided to attempt a recovery in the Adirondack Mountains, as the Adirondack climate was renowned for its restorative properties. His first move was to the Paul Smith's Hotel, where he stayed until he moved his family to Saranac Lake in 1876. There he founded the Adirondack Cottage Sanitarium, where he set up a practice for local patients with TB and other ailments. This facility was burned down in a fire in 1894.

Dr. Trudeau was not one to permit adversity to keep him down. He had already suffered through the loss of his brother to tuberculosis and would later lose three of his four children to various diseases. He persevered until he was able to raise funds to open the Saranac Laboratory for the Study of Tuberculosis. In 1894, this was the first laboratory in the United States dedicated to the study of this disease.

Dr. Trudeau went on to practice in Saranac Lake, attempting several times to return to the New York City region, which resulted in recurrences of his original disease. He found that he was able to cure many cases of tuberculosis with a combination of fresh Adirondack air, recuperative rest, and a healthy, balanced diet. He also collaborated with other scientists around the world to discover that the disease was caused by a microorganism, the tubercle bacillus. As mentioned earlier, a long-term and permanent cure would not be available until the discovery of penicillin.

The exhibits in the laboratory museum are spread out over the basement and first floor. On display are a great many instruments and glassware pieces used by Dr. Trudeau in his experimentations on the disease. There are information boards that explain the problems and progress he encountered as he performed his research.

The Saranac Laboratory was closed in 1966 and was transferred to Paul Smith's College. Ownership was later transferred to Historic Saranac Lake in 1998. It was then fully restored and reopened as the current museum in 2009.

The museum is open to the public from Tuesday through Saturday, 10:00 a.m.–5:00 p.m.

Part of the laboratory, main floor. On display are numerous pieces of glassware and instruments used by Dr. Trudeau.
PHOTO BY LARRY WEILL

It is closed on Sunday and Monday. Admission is $7.00 for adults and $5.00 for students. Children under age 12 are admitted free.

The museum is located at 89 Church Street in Saranac Lake, which is a two-minute walk from the Hotel Saranac. The phone number is 518-891-4606, or visit https://www.historicsaranaclake.org.

WHERE THE FISH COME FROM!

Have you ever caught a real "whopper" of a fish and wondered just where it originated? Did that hefty landlocked salmon really swim up a stream to get to your favorite fishing hole?

If you and your children ever wanted to learn more about the game fish that live in the waters of the Adirondacks, then the Adirondack Fish Culture Station is the place for you. Located down a side road

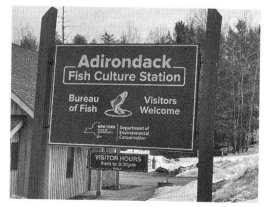

Sign in front of the DEC's Fish Culture Station in Saranac Lake.
PHOTO BY LARRY WEILL

on the outskirts of Saranac Lake, New York, it provides the complete story of how New York's game fish are bred and distributed. It's a great place to visit and learn, even if you aren't an angler.

The station has a visitors' center with a bevy of displays, a fish pool, fish identification posters, and a video projection area for watching educational fish-related videos. There are also a number of trophy fish of different varieties mounted on the walls of the room.

Visitor's center room with fish pool and multiple displays and informational posters.
PHOTO BY LARRY WEILL

Moving from the front room to the back building, visitors are treated to a view of the massive breeding efforts conducted by the state to enhance our sports anglers' experience. The room is used to breed Atlantic landlocked salmon, the only such facility in the state of New York. The landlocked salmon bred here are used to stock bodies of water all over New York in such diverse locations as Lake Ontario, Skaneateles Lake, Lake George, Cayuga Lake, Blue Mountain Lake, Lake Champlain, and Schroon Lake. It is truly a sight to behold!

This rear building, called the Production Building, is a very long arrangement of 16 fish holding tanks, each filled with differing numbers of younger-versus-older landlocked salmon. The tanks are large, with each holding about 17,000 gallons of water that is constantly being pumped into the tank, with an inflow of fresh water at 125 gallons per minute.

View looking along the 16 fish holding tanks in the Production Building.
PHOTO BY LARRY WEILL

Each of the 16 tanks is used to house a different age group of the salmon fry. Some of these pools are for very young "yearlings" and may contain up to 18,000 of the immature fish. By the time the fry have reached one year old, they are reduced to about 1,000 per tank. They are further reduced to 300 per tank at three years, and 150 per tank at five years. The fish in the latter tanks are truly impressive in length and girth. (The author of this book only wishes he'd have hooked into one of these monsters at any time in his life!)

The fish in these tanks are used not only for stocking but also for producing fertilized eggs for the next generation of fish fry. The life cycle and distribution of these landlocked salmon is explained in a superb video that is available for viewing in the visitors' center room up front.

The fish hatchery facility is located at 103 Fish Hatchery Road (right off NY Route 30) in Saranac Lake, New York. According to the website, it is open from 9:00 a.m. until 4:00 p.m. daily from April through November. However, the sign on the door says "closed at 3:30 p.m.," so you might want to plan accordingly. There is no fee for admittance, and anyone interested in fishing would find this facility of interest.

SIX NATIONS IROQUOIS CULTURAL CENTER

The Adirondack Park is full of mountains, lakes, and towns bearing Native American names. The history of Native Americans inside the Blue Line dates back thousands of years, with much of that history predating the written record.

One thing that is certain is that the six tribes of the Iroquois Nation have resided in the region for as long as humans have called this part of the country "home." Artifacts dating back several millennia have turned up in archaeological digs across the state, as well as at random construction excavation sites. Preserving and cataloging these finds has always represented a challenge to those interested in the state's antiquities.

Six Nations Iroquois Cultural Center in Onchiota.
PHOTO BY LARRY WEILL

One of the region's most interesting but least known facilities for preserving the past is found in the small community of Onchiota, located in the middle of Franklin County. It was there, in 1954, that Ray Fadden built the first two rooms of what would become the Six Nations Iroquois Cultural Center. As stated at the center's website, the timber used to build those first rooms was milled locally from trees felled by Ray Fadden.

"Ray was a teacher who taught on reservations all over the state," said Dave Fadden, one of Ray's grandsons. "This property was originally used as a camp before Ray built the original two rooms of the museum. Shortly thereafter, he and his wife moved here full time. Their son, John, was also a teacher, and he too created a lot of what you see here today."

John's two sons, Dave and Don Fadden, both run the Cultural Center today and have overseen its growth and expansion to its current size. As Dave stated, "The main goal of the Center is to preserve and display as much of the Iroquois culture as possible to the young people, and to help wipe out improper misconceptions and stereotypes."

Dave spoke for quite a while about the growth of the museum and other topics of interest regarding the Native American history of the region. His sincere pride in his ancestors and their role in the state is evident in his voice.

Brothers Dave (left) and Don (right) Fadden, who own and operate the Six Nations Iroquois Cultural Center.
Photo by Larry Weill

The center is filled with exhibits of Iroquois art, jewelry, clothing, pottery, and *lots* more. Additionally, records and books stored in the rooms document more modern times, when events were recorded for future generations to read. Of particular interest is a large poster that lists the names of over 2,000 Iroquois residents of various tribal reservations who fought on or contributed to the American side in World War II. "Included in that list are the names of at least two 'Code Talkers,' known for communicating in their native tongues to help preserve the secrecy of our troops' movements. Most of these warriors did not even tell their own families about their actions until many years after the war," said Dave.

The museum has finally received some of the recognition it has deserved, including designation as a nonprofit organization and receiving grants to help with the expansion projects planned by the Faddens. "We've acquired 300 acres of land up the road from our current building," said Dave. "There, we will build a new facility with three times the space that can handle more events, festivals, and exhibits. We've also fostered partnerships with the Wild Center in Tupper Lake, as well as other organizations, and helped design exhibits for their visitors." (Both Dave and Don are superbly talented artists who use their skills to produce impressive works of art.)

The Six Nations Iroquois Cultural Center is located at 1462 County Route 60 in Onchiota, New York. The phone number is 518-891-2299, or visit www.6nicc.com. The hours are posted online.

ALMANZO WILDER FARM

The Almanzo Wilder Farm is a working museum on a backcountry road, seemingly in the middle of nowhere. It is celebrated primarily because of the fame of Almanzo's literary wife, Laura Ingalls Wilder, who authored (among other volumes) the book *Farmer Boy*. The farmhouse is famous because it is the only "Little House" building that still stands on its original site.

The rectangular red farmhouse was started by Almanzo Wilder's father, James Wilder, in

Birthplace of Almanzo Wilder, husband of Laura Ingalls Wilder, in Burke.
PHOTO BY LARRY WEILL

1840. James was one of 10 children born to Abel and Hannah Wilder, who moved to the state from Bridport, Vermont, in 1817. Almanzo was born in 1857 and moved with the family to Spring Valley, Minnesota, in 1875, when he was 18.

Laura Ingalls Wilder is famous for writing all nine of the Little House on the Prairie books, although only the second volume in this series had anything to do with the farm. (The second book was written about Almanzo's life.) Each of the nine books was written about a different location.

On the day of my visit, I was guided through the buildings by Donna Johnson, who serves as the treasurer for the Almanzo & Laura Ingalls Wilder Association in addition to providing in-depth tours to visitors. She has been with the farm since 2014 and has accumulated a wealth of knowledge about the property.

"The Almanzo & Laura Ingalls Wilder Association was started in 1986, and the property was purchased in 1987," said Johnson. "The house and buildings sit on 84 of the original 88 acres of land. The house itself was in very rough shape and took a couple years to restore to its current condition."

With the exception of the farmhouse, all the other buildings have been recreated. The last of the barns, which were built by previous owners, had burned down in the late 1960s. The reconstruction of the new barn was started in 1994 by Michael Brand, a superbly talented local builder, who worked for eight years using Almanzo's original sketches as well as findings from archaeological digs conducted in 1988–1989 to meticulously recreate the structure sites described in Laura Ingalls Wilder's book series.

Barn buildings on the site, all of which have recreational uses. The original barns were lost to a fire in 1969.

PHOTO BY LARRY WEILL

112

Dining room inside the farmhouse. Almost all the contents were donated by private donors.

PHOTO BY LARRY WEILL

"The television show helped this site get a foothold in people's imaginations. Some of our visitors have been to all nine of the sites mentioned in the *Little House* series. Oftentimes, they either begin or end their journeys at the Wilder Homestead."

Visitors to the Almanzo Wilder Farm can tour the farmhouse, the barns, and a one-room schoolhouse that has been added to the site. (The schoolhouse was never part of the original property. It was framed by Michael Brand and finished by volunteers in 2011–2013.) The museum is a popular place for tourists and usually receives at least 5,000 visitors in an average year. This includes travelers from all 50 states as well as from 15 to 20 countries around the world.

General admission to the farm is $14.00. Seniors are $13.00, and youths ages 6–16 are $8.00. Children below age 6 are free.

If you would like to visit this fascinating historical site, it is located at 177 Stacy Road, Burke, New York. The mailing address is PO Box 283, Malone, New York 12953. The phone number is 518-483-1207, or visit farm@almanzowilderfarm.com.

ATTRACTIONS OF FULTON COUNTY

THE UNION HALL INN RESTAURANT

The town of Johnstown, New York, in Fulton County, is steeped in history dating back to the inception of our country. One of the more recognized local buildings still in use since the 1700s is the Union Hall Inn Restaurant (then known as the de FonClaire Inn), which was built in 1798 by Vaumane Jean Baptiste de FonClaire, a captain in the French Army.

The inn was a popular stopping point for travelers, as well as for the local residents of the area. The barroom was originally located in the basement of the building, although that room no longer exists today. According to Kim Henck, one of the current owners, the basement taproom was demolished 100 years ago and is now a boiler room.

Union Hall Inn Restaurant on Union Place in Johnstown.
PHOTO BY LARRY WEILL

One of the more notable personalities of the day who frequented this pub was Nicholas Stoner, a veteran of the Revolutionary War and of battles against Native Americans and a well-known hunter and trapper. Nicholas's father, Henry Stoner, also served in the Revolutionary War, later settling near current-day Amsterdam. He was attacked and killed by a band of Native Americans in 1782, which would eventually lead to a link with the Union Hall Inn. It was there (sometime in the early 1800s), in the basement of the inn, that Nicholas Stoner overheard a Native American man talking about how he had slain Nicholas's father some 20 years earlier. Stoner instantly became enraged and flung a red-hot fire iron at the man, who was mortally wounded. The local sheriff arrested Stoner, but his veteran friends broke him out of jail, and he was never prosecuted.

Note: During my visit I asked to see the room where the aforementioned incident took place, but this all happened in the original taproom, which is now gone.

Another famous character of the day who was an early patron of the Union Hall Inn was Joseph Bonaparte, brother of Napoleon. Joseph held many titles in Europe that were bestowed upon him by his more-famous brother, including king of Spain. However, following Napoleon's defeat at Waterloo, Joseph moved

UNION HALL   JOHNSTOWN, N.Y.
Union Hall was built in 1798 by Captain Fon Clair & has been used as a tavern & also a private home. Nick Stoner is said to have killed an Indian there & Napoleon's brother Joseph stopped there on the way to his camp.

Early etching of the original Union Hall Inn building.
PHOTO BY LARRY WEILL

across the ocean to the United States and took up residence near Philadelphia. He also owned a large tract of land in the Adirondacks.

The current inn, which operates as a restaurant and barroom, is owned by the husband and wife team of Kim and Anne Henck, who purchased the historic establishment in 1905. Their daughter, Megan (a Culinary Institute graduate), contributes to the menu development in the kitchen.

As a side note, the author had the wonderful experience of dining at the Union Hall Inn Restaurant and speaking with the owners at length. While this text is not meant to serve as a restaurant guide, I would be remiss if I did not say that I enjoyed my meal to its fullest extent. The food itself was wonderfully prepared, and everyone associated with the restaurant was incredibly friendly. I could summarize it perfectly by saying that the Union Hall Inn Restaurant gives you a little taste of history that tastes amazingly good.

The address is 2 Union Place, Johnstown, New York, and the phone number is 518-762-3210. Hours of operation are Tuesday through Saturday, 5 p.m.– 9 p.m. It is also open for lunch on Thursday from 11:30 a.m.–2 p.m. Closed on Sunday and Monday.

EARLY TALES OF MURDER: ELIZABETH VAN VALKENBURGH

This morbid bit of Adirondack history is preserved through its few remaining artifacts, which rest in the Fulton County Museum in Gloversville, New York. Elizabeth Van Valkenburgh was born in Bennington, Vermont, in 1799, but was orphaned at an early age and moved to Cambridge, New York. She married at age 20 and had four children with her allegedly abusive husband, who moved the family to Pennsylvania and then back again to a residence near Johnstown, New York. It was there that she resorted to murder, adding arsenic to his rum, a crime to which she later confessed.

Elizabeth married again in 1834, this time to John Van Valkenburgh, with whom she had two additional children. However, she claimed that her husband was "addicted to liquor" and subjected both herself and their children to severe hardships. She again used arsenic as her poison of choice, adding it to her husband's tea in March 1845. John died within a week.

Portable gallows used to hang Elizabeth Van Valkenburgh.
PHOTO BY LARRY WEILL

Photograph of the jail and courthouse where Van Valkenburgh was imprisoned and put on trial, in Johnstown.
PHOTO BY LARRY WEILL

Elizabeth's misdeeds were discovered, and she learned that she was to be arrested and tried for her crimes. She fled from her homestead and went into hiding but was soon arrested after sustaining a severe fall with significant injuries. (It has been debated whether she broke her hip or her leg in the fall. Regardless, her injuries prevented her from ever walking again.) She was convicted of murder and sentenced to be executed by hanging. Her execution was extremely unusual in that she was carried to a portable gallows in her rocking chair, in which she sat until the gallows door was released and she fell to her death.

The portable gallows used to perform Elizabeth Van Valkenburgh's execution is on permanent display at the Fulton County Museum, at 237 Kingsboro Avenue, Gloversville, New York. Summer hours are Thursday to Sunday noon–4 p.m. The phone number is 518-725-2203.

The museum is only open on select days and hours. Check its seasonal hours by calling (518) 725-2203 or online at https://www.facebook.com/fultoncomuseum/.

THE TRAVELING (*BRONCO BUSTER*) SCULPTURE

Frederic Sackrider Remington is a name that is probably much more widely recognized among art enthusiasts in this country than by fans of the Adirondacks. Remington was one of the foremost American artists, having lived between 1861 and 1909. His father served as a colonel during the Civil War but is probably better known for founding the Remington Arms Company.

Although Remington displayed early signs of artistic talent, he didn't pursue it in his early studies. He gravitated toward art after his father passed away. His earlier works were paintings and illustrations, mostly depicting scenes from the American West.

Remington was in his mid-thirties when he took up sculpting. His very first piece, *Bronco Buster*, became an American classic that established him as one of America's leading artists. An original cast of this very same sculpture can be found in the Oval Office of the White House, a gift received during the Carter administration.

Remington's wife, Eva Caten, was born in a small town near Syracuse in 1859. Her father had business ties (through the railroad industry) to Gloversville, and the family lived there in later years. Because of her Gloversville connection, Eva donated a cast of the *Bronco Buster* statue to the local Gloversville Library in 1919, where it resided for 13 years until it was stolen in 1932.

The trail of the missing sculpture went cold for many years. While the police had a lead on the suspected thief, and he was eventually arrested (although for a different crime), he managed to escape from confinement, and the library was unable to recover the pilfered art.

The story then winds its way through a number of sales and acquisitions, as the stolen *Bronco Buster* cast was passed between owners no fewer than four times before it was purchased by a collector in New York City. The new owner had happened to read a story about the stolen piece of art and canceled the sale

Public Library in Gloversville, home of the *Bronco Buster* sculpture.
PHOTO BY LARRY WEILL

in mid-transaction. He simultaneously contacted the law enforcement authorities in Fulton County, who facilitated the return of the sculpture to the library in Gloversville.

The *Bronco Buster* is now on permanent display in the main room of the Gloversville Library, locked securely in a display case for all to see. Hopefully, its traveling days are now over.

The Gloversville Library is located at 58 E Fulton Street, Gloversville, New York. The phone number is 518-725-2819. Hours of operation are Monday 2 p.m.–7 p.m., Tuesday to Thursday 9 a.m.–7 p.m., and Friday 9 a.m.–5 p.m. The library is closed on Saturday and Sunday.

THE WORLD'S LARGEST GLOVE

While performing the research for this book, the author came across hundreds of possible subjects, ranging from the historical to the unusual to the simply bizarre. So when Samantha Hall-Saladino, the Fulton County historian, mentioned that the county museum in Gloversville was home to the world's largest glove, it instantly became a "must see" addition to this book.

Dale Brown, volunteer at the Fulton County Museum in Gloversville, standing next to the world's largest glove.
PHOTO BY LARRY WEILL

The glove itself sits in a leather-themed room in the back of the museum's first floor. Surrounded by numerous other, more normal-sized gloves, it easily dwarfs its companions in the display case. Standing at an estimated 4 feet in height, the glove is impressive by any standards. It is also perfectly proportioned and would fit almost any hand if shrunk uniformly from top to bottom.

"There's really not much we can tell you on the origins of this piece," said Dale Brown, the museum volunteer who led the author through this exhibit. "We can only speculate that it was created to be a display piece for people to see at different fairs and promotions around the area. We believe it was created sometime around the 1940s, but we can't even be sure of that."

A quick check with local reference libraries adds even more intrigue to the mystery, as the glove was supposedly created by the Walker La Rowe Glove Company in Northville, New York. Yet the "Hide and Leather" issue of *International Weekly Review*, dated October 1, 1921, reported that the Larowe Glove Company was "recently dissolved." (It is possible that the Walker La Rowe Glove Company was a separate entity from the Larowe Glove Company, although an exhaustive search of the businesses of that era was not conducted.) If these dates are correct, then the glove was either created sometime prior to the 1920s, or another manufacturer had a hand (not literally) in its creation.

The glove, surrounded by dozens of normal-sized pieces in the display.
PHOTO BY LARRY WEILL

The exhibit of gloves and other leather apparel is a natural fit for Gloversville, which at one time served as the home for over 200 glove manufacturers. At one point in the latter half of the 1800s, almost 80 percent of the people residing in and around Gloversville worked in the glove and leather business, making it the largest business and employer in the region.

The Fulton County Museum has hours that vary throughout the year. Summer hours are Thursday to Sunday noon–4 p.m. The address is 237 Kingsboro Avenue, Gloversville, New York, and the phone number is 518-725-2203.

For more details, visit online at http://www.cityofgloversville.com/fulton-county-museum/.

THE KNOX MANSION AND LEGACY

The large white mansion that sits off of West 2nd Avenue in Johnstown has a long and storied past. Built in 1889, it served as the residence for Charles B. Knox, who owned and operated the Knox Gelatin Factory in Johnstown. Originally employed as a glove salesman, Knox supposedly got the idea to produce gelatin while watching his wife work with the substance in their Gloversville home.

Charles Knox ran the successful business until his death in 1908, at which time his wife, Rose, assumed the leadership role. Women were seldom seen as heads of corporations in that era, and many people (including her own employees) doubted her ability to lead the business. However, Rose was more than up

The Knox Mansion on West 2nd Avenue in Johnstown.
Photo by Larry Weill

to the task, and immediately turned heads with her visionary ideas for corporate management.

Rose and her husband had always been very close, and he undoubtedly shared many of his thoughts and ideas with his wife. But Rose had many of her own ideas, and she expressed these as soon as she took over the company. Her first move was to order the elimination of the "back door entrance" to the factory for female employees. She considered everyone to be equal and declared that everyone would enter through the same door.

A progressive thinker, she instituted many programs for employees that would become hallmarks of American business, including the five-day workweek and the introduction of paid vacations for all. Her innovative policies and sound financial management resulted in the Knox Gelatin Company making it through the hard times of the Great Depression without having to lay off any employees.

The old Knox Mansion, which had previously fallen into a sad state of disrepair, was purchased in 1993 by Marty Quinn, who has worked to improve the historic building ever since. Repairs were needed to fix the roofs, ceilings, plumbing, wiring, and more.

The 42-room mansion has a great many features not found in most houses of that era, including an elevator, central vacuum, and solid lava ash fireplace, which Rose Knox reportedly imported from an Italian castle at a cost of $200,000.

One thing that fascinates most visitors is that the building is supposedly haunted. One of its later owners, a physician, supposedly died within its walls, and a gardener who worked on the grounds for close to 30 years has also announced his presence to the occasional visitor. Reports of supernatural events, including doors opening and closing, music coming from empty rooms, voices, and items falling off shelves are commonplace. Also unusual in this residence are several hidden doors and rooms and an eerie cellar with multiple floors.

Visitors interested in touring parts of the Knox Mansion, which is now operated as a nonprofit history museum, can find it at 104 West 2nd Avenue, Johnstown, New York. The phone number is 518-752-8231, or visit online at https://www.facebook.com/knoxmansion13/. It is also open to the public on Halloween.

GRAVESITE OF SIR WILLIAM JOHNSON

Sir William Johnson, 1st Baronet, was undoubtedly one of the most influential men in the area that would later become Fulton County. Born in Ireland in 1715, he moved to what later became New York State around 1738 to assist in managing his family's real estate assets, which were situated within the territory of the Mohawks.

St. John's Episcopal Church in Johnstown, the site of Sir William Johnson's grave.
PHOTO BY LARRY WEILL

Johnson's uncle, Peter Warren, had originally purchased a large tract of land in the area around modern-day Warrensburgh, which is where he intended his nephew to settle and establish a fledgling community. However, Johnson recognized greater opportunities farther north, where he could better profit from the fur trade routes between Albany and New York City. In this region, he became accepted and welcomed by the Mohawks, one of the Six Nations of the Iroquois.

Johnson's exploits were numerous and fabled, and he was fortunate to possess great influence with both the Mohawks and the British government. Having been appointed an honorary Mohawk chief in early 1740, he later ascended to the positions of "New York Agent to the Iroquois (in 1746), Colonel of the Warrior of the Six Nations, and British Superintendent of Indian Affairs (1756)."

Johnson was later commissioned as a major general by the British and asked to lead forces against the French fort at Crown Point. Johnson was recognized for maintaining his position (if not for outright victory) at the Battle of Lake George, for which the British Parliament and King George III officially made him a baronet.

Johnson subsequently died of a stroke in 1774 and was buried with much fanfare beneath the altar of St. John's Episcopal Church in Johnstown. This was

Colonial-era depiction of Sir William Johnson, 1st Baronet.
PHOTO BY LARRY WEILL

Gravestone of Sir William Johnson outside St. John's Episcopal Church.
PHOTO BY LARRY WEILL

actually the second church that stood at that site, and it later burned down in a fire in November 1836.

When the process of rebuilding the new (current) church commenced the following year (1837), the grave of the baronet was lost and then forgotten, as the base of the new building was not on the same foundational footprint. It was later located by Reverend Kellogg, who sealed and marked the gravesite in 1862.

Visitors to the church can visit the gravesite of this amazing colonist in the front yard of St. John's Episcopal Church. It is marked with a gravestone and a series of plaques commemorating his life and exploits. The church is located at 1 North Market Street, Johnstown, New York, and is always open to the public.

MOUNTAIN LAKE TRAIN CAR WRECK OF 1902

Almost no one knows about the town of Bleecker, New York, even many of those who live inside the Adirondack Park itself. A stone's throw from Johnstown, it has fewer than a thousand residents and very few commercial interests. Yet this name loomed quite large in the early days of the twentieth century due to a horrible accident that took place inside its borders. The tragedy took the lives of 14 travelers, all of whom had been taking part in Fourth of July festivities on top of the mountain, which included fireworks and other celebrations.

The electric train wreck on the side of
Bleecker Mountain in 1902.
Photo by Larry Weill

Artifacts left over from the wreck on
Bleecker Mountain.
Photo by Larry Weill

The bend in the mountain road where the
train cars came to rest.
Photo by Larry Weill

According to the accounts of
local historians and train company ex-
ecutives, the event was the combined
result of human error and equipment
failure. Two cars of the Mountain
Lake Railroad were descending when
a series of events caused an open car
carrying approximately 55 passengers
to be struck by a heavier, closed car
carrying an additional 70 revelers.
The collision caused both cars to
shoot down the rails toward a sharply
curved corner at excessive speed.
Upon reaching the corner, both cars
jumped the tracks, and dozens of passengers were thrown from the open
trolley cars. Many were crushed beneath the heavier car and were killed
or suffered excruciating injuries. All
told, 14 people were killed and another 60 were injured in the crash.

Following investigations discovered that excessive speed, insuf-
ficient brakes for the weather, and
inadequate intervals between the departure of the cars were all contribut-
ing factors to the disaster. The tally of
deaths and injuries might have been
even worse if not for the quick thinking of a 17-year-old crash victim,
who sprinted back up the tracks and
warned the next car coming down the
line to apply its brakes.

The railroad closed permanently in 1918, and a railroad history
group was able to find a few pieces
of hardware and wire as late as 2013.
The author rode along Mountain
Lake South Shore Road in 2019 in
a fruitless attempt to locate any vis-

ible remains of the crash. A gate now bars the end of the road, sealing off access to the site. Further attempts at the discovery of additional remains are not recommended.

Exhibits about this event, including an actual length of the train rail, can be viewed at the Fulton County Museum, located at 237 Kingsboro Avenue, Gloversville, New York. Summer hours are Thursday to Sunday, noon–4 p.m. The phone number is 518-725-2203. Museum hours vary throughout the year. For more details, visit the museum's website at http://www.cityofgloversville.com/fulton-county-museum/.

GREAT SACANDAGA LAKE FISH

To campers and hikers who pass through the Adirondack wilderness, any fish that surpasses the one-pound mark is a whopper. Brook trout, which comprise the majority of the real backwoods fish stock, seldom go over that weight in the remote lakes, although those who are lucky enough to hook into a lake trout can walk away with fish that are 10–20 times that size.

The northern pike that inhabit the cold waters of the Adirondacks (and other northern lakes) can reach truly astounding proportions, as witnessed by one Peter DuBuc, who was fishing in the Great Sacandaga Lake on September 15, 1940. Peter DuBuc was no amateur angler, having already landed some colossal members of the trout and bass families across the region. A largemouth bass he landed in 1940 tied the New York State record for that category.

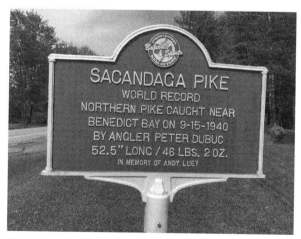

Sign commemorating Peter DuBuc's 1940 record-setting northern pike, caught in September 1940.
Photo by Larry Weill

On the morning of September 15, 1940, DuBuc was trolling the waters of a quiet bay on the Great Sacandaga Lake, as described in an article written by Ben East, a reporter for *Outdoor Life Magazine*, in 1959. DuBuc was fishing in about 10 feet of water, in an area that still contained many of the tree stumps left when the grounds were flooded to create the lake in 1930.

DuBuc was lucky (or knowledgeable) enough to have 300 feet of strong line on his reel and a sturdy bronze leader that would hold up to the strong, aggressive, and weighty fish. Even with the equipment in his boat and the right know-how, it still took him a full hour to land the whopper. He quickly recognized that it was a record-worthy catch. According to the 1959 *Outdoor Life* article, he had it weighed twice: "Once in the town of Broadalbin, then again in Albany on beam scales both times." The fish weighed in at 46 pounds, 2 ounces. It was 52½ inches long, with a 25-inch girth.

The fish stood as a world record for over 40 years, until a 55 pounder was caught in the waters of Greffern Lake, West Germany, in 1986. Peter DuBuc died in 1970, at the age of 80. At the time of his death, his 1940 catch still held the world record.

Today, the fish can be viewed on display at the Fulton County Museum at 237 Kingsboro Avenue, Gloversville, New York. Summer hours are Thursday to Sunday, noon–4 p.m. The phone number is 518-725-2203.

GHOST AT NINE CORNER LAKE

Nine Corner Lake is a remote body of water that can be visited via a hiking trail, which begins on NY Route 29A near its junction with NY Route 10 in the town of Caroga. It is a quiet, peaceful place that significantly contrasts with an undated story from long ago.

Back in the heyday of the lumber industry, a house used to stand on the roadway that passed closest to this oddly shaped body of water. The owner of the house used to rent rooms to the various lumberjacks and other men of the woods. The tenants included a number of French Canadians, who were well represented throughout the lumber camps of the Adirondacks.

According to the mostly forgotten legend, a group of 11 of these Frenchmen were engaged in a bark-peeling job centered on the west side of Nine Corner Lake. Friendly and good-natured, they were well received by the townsfolk of the area.

One afternoon, as the men were returning in a small boat from the other shoreline, a quick-moving storm overtook them on the lake. The thunder and lightning were severe, with high winds and hellacious rains. The boat was pushed wildly over the bucking waves with no regard for direction. It is unknown whether any of the passengers could swim.

Later that evening, the landlord of the boardinghouse became alarmed when none of the logging group had returned. By the following morning, a search party was formed to locate any of the French Canadians who might have survived the ordeal. They quickly found the remains of the boat, which had evidently smashed against some rocks and had a large hole in the bottom. Soon after that, they came across the sunken bodies of the drowned lumberjacks, which had been strewn across the bottom of the lake. It was a horrible scene; the rescue crew did their best to retrieve the bodies and bring them back to the boardinghouse.

According to the story, two hunters were working the land west of Nine Corner Lake some years later when a violent thunderstorm moved into the area. Eager to escape from the thunder and bolts of lightning, they began to run along the lake's southern shore toward shelter. During one prolonged flash of lightning, they were horrified to witness a boat overturned on the white-capped lake, to which clung a drowning band of lumberjacks.

This story has been repeated by numerous individuals over the years. Some have reported hearing the distressed screams of those very same men, calling for help before sinking to their watery graves. It is an oft-repeated tale in the area around Canada Lake, although there is little in the written history of the region to document the original story. The only recorded version of this tale comes from a Little Falls newspaper dated somewhere around 1900.

The lake can be reached via a 0.9-mile trail from Route 29A, about 0.1 mile west of Route 10. If you decide to visit, please watch out for storms. And ghosts.

FAMOUS TRIALS AT THE STATE'S OLDEST COURTHOUSE

Even those familiar with the geography of New York and its 62 counties are sometimes baffled by this question: Where the heck is Tryon County? To properly answer this riddle requires a knowledge of the state's history, as Tryon County only existed in name from 1772 until 1784, when it was renamed Montgomery County. Named after William Tryon, the provincial (pre–Revolutionary War) governor of the state, it listed Johnstown as its county seat. Tryon County, along with Charlotte County, were both huge in terms of land, occupying most of present-day Upstate New York, from the Mohawk River to the Canadian border.

Construction of the Tryon County Courthouse was started in 1772, although there are records of its continuing phases of completion continuing through at least 1775. Sir William Johnson not only oversaw the building, but

Fulton County Courthouse, originally known as the Tryon
County Courthouse, in Johnstown.
PHOTO BY LARRY WEILL

also contributed a significant portion of the overall costs for the structure. (According to early records, he also pitched in 25 gallons of rum to maintain the high morale and spirits of the men involved in the construction.)

The courthouse has been the scene of several famous trials over the years, perhaps none more famous than that of Solomon Southwick, a businessman who was accused by State Assembly Speaker Alexander Sheldon of attempted bribery. According to Sheldon, Southwick had tried to provide monetary compensation in exchange for his influence in the incorporation of a large bank in New York City. The trial drew attention not only for its importance and scope, but because one of the defense attorneys hired by Southwick was none other than Aaron Burr.

Burr had gained notoriety not only for killing Alexander Hamilton in 1804, but also for the high crime of treason in 1807, of which he was acquitted. Burr, working with a team of three other attorneys, successfully defended Southwick and won him an acquittal in the case.

This historic building was later renamed the Montgomery County Courthouse, and then (since 1838) the Fulton County Courthouse. It has undergone numerous improvements and upgrades over the years, necessary to meet modern-day sanitary and business requirements. As stated on the historical marker in front, it is the only provincial courthouse still in use in New York State today.

The building is located at 223 W. Main Street in Johnstown, New York. Access to the building may be restricted, as it is still used as a functioning courthouse. However, the courthouse is next to St. John's Episcopal Church, which also houses the burial site of Sir William Johnson. Historical markers and numerous signboards with additional information are also available to those who visit the site.

THERE'S AN OSTRICH IN MY CAR!

Most visitors to the Adirondacks are interested in encountering the wildlife that abounds throughout the park. This usually includes anything from beaver and porcupine to white-tailed deer, and even an occasional moose. However, there is one location inside the Blue Line where that list of critters expands to include many more, and it's definitely worth a visit.

Sign at the entrance of Adirondack Animal Land in Gloversville, which welcomes families during July and August. PHOTO BY LARRY WEILL

Adirondack Animal Land is a unique attraction that appeals to both young and old alike. It is a large tract of land that is set up as a breeding facility for over 500 animals of various sizes and origins. Located at 3554 NY-30, Gloversville, New York, the facility offers visitors an easy way to drive through the parklike setting and view dozens of animal species. The phone number is 518-883-5748.

Sighting the furry inhabitants of this facility is not difficult. As a matter of fact, you will have no choice. As soon as you turn onto the entrance road, your car will most likely be approached by curious mammals and ratites, which is a fancy name for a group of large, flightless birds that includes ostriches and emus, among others. While these animals are unique and appear friendly, one of the first rules of the park is to *stay inside your car*. An ostrich is capable of killing a human with a single kick and may perceive you as a threat, provoking an attack.

While there are parts of the facility that permit family members to exit their cars and feed caged animals, most visitors simply drive along the looping road that passes through the grounds. Along that road you can view a great many of the different species that are bred and raised at the facility. You can also purchase cups of feed to give to some of the animals if you care to interact on a more intimate basis.

The length of your tour through the facility can vary greatly, not only based on the car traffic on the road but

Mother zebra standing above her young offspring at Animal Land. PHOTO BY LARRY WEILL

also on the cooperation of the animals themselves. There are times when a deer or alpaca or sheep may be stubborn about moving across the road and create its own traffic jam. As the rules point out, "the animals have the right of way," so things can get a bit backed up when this happens.

There are a number of things you need to know while planning a trip to Adirondack Animal Land. First, it's only fully open to the public in July and August each year, although the facility does conduct prearranged school visits during the month of June.

Entrance to the park (and gift shop purchases) is by cash only. Credit cards are not accepted at this facility. However, there is an ATM machine on the grounds. Another thing you need to know is that dogs are *not* welcome inside the park, as they can scare the resident animals, so please leave them at home when you visit. No convertibles are permitted, and any "configurable" vehicles (e.g., Jeeps) must have doors and a top installed prior to entry. Animal Land is not responsible for any damage to a visitor's vehicle incurred through animal activity. Also, visitors are only permitted to feed the animals food that is purchased at the facility.

The park is open in July and August at 10:00 a.m. daily, and final admission is at 3:00 p.m. (closing time is 4:00 p.m.). Adult tickets are $18.00, and children's tickets (ages 2–12) are $16.00. Children under age two are free. For more information, visit https://adirondackanimalland.com.

Pair of bison resting near the back of Animal Land.

THE THEATER THAT FITS LIKE A GLOVE

Movie theaters have evolved substantially since the early days of the silver screen. Patrons of the original movie houses would hardly recognize the modern-day cinemas, with their reclining lounge seats and Dolby surround-sound speaker systems.

One of the most amazing surviving examples of an early theater sits on North Main Street in the city of Gloversville, New York. The Glove was opened in 1914 and was one of the original vaudeville houses. Mike Maricondi, who today serves as the general manager of the Glove Theatre, explained how the venue transitioned from vaudeville to its later uses.

"Soon after the theater was completed, it was acquired by the Schine family, who owned several similar movie houses. They used it for both movies as well as Vaudeville acts. Sometimes they did both on the same day with other live acts in between," explained Maricondi. "In the 1930s they moved to presenting solely movies. People who wanted to attend the show could go to McClellan's drug store, where they could get a free ticket to the movies with the purchase of a soda. It was cheap entertainment for the town."

Somewhere around 1975, the Glove Theatre ceased operation and shuttered its doors. That began an extended period of vacancy during which the building and its contents deteriorated. No one entered the structure for years, and it continued its downward spiral. By 1995, the city of Gloversville was ready to tear down the place and replace it with a parking lot. That's when Mayor Vince DeSantis stepped in and founded a volunteer board that purchased the building for the price of one dollar.

The historic Glove Theatre on North Main Street in Gloversville.

PHOTO BY LARRY WEILL

Mike Maricondi standing behind the Glove Theatre concession stand.

PHOTO BY LARRY WEILL

Upon entering the long-abandoned building, the local group were astounded at the level of damage and decay inside. The ceiling had caved into the seating area, and there was a lot of water on the floor. The seats were ruined as well and needed to be removed and discarded. It was obvious that a great amount of work was required to restore the facility, which was dubbed the Glove Performing Arts Center (GPAC).

Much of the restoration was undertaken in the early 2000s, including pumping out the water and rebuilding the ceiling. Soon thereafter, the Glove reopened to conduct events such as children's musicals and community concerts. The venue was shut down once again during the COVID-19 pandemic, but it reopened in August 2021. Since then it has continued to operate at least one day each week, and the movies are open to the public and free of charge. (The theater operates as a 501(c)3 nonprofit.)

Maricondi is proud of the work that he and his band of volunteers have accomplished. Working with just a facilities manager (David LaMonica), a board of nine dedicated members, and about 30 to 50 local volunteers, they have truly worked wonders. Additionally, some much-needed state grant money and contributions from a few major local benefactors have been put to good use restoring the ceiling and covering the walls with materials to greatly improve the acoustics. Further projects include completing work on the walls, as well as improving the balcony, installing a fire sprinkler system, and bolstering the air conditioning for the warmer months.

For more information on the Glove Theatre, visit its website at https://theglovetheatre.com. If you wish to donate to the cause of supporting the theater, there is a "Donate" button near the bottom of the home page. But no matter what, stop in sometime and see how theaters looked in the early days of the last century.

View of the seating area and stage looking down from the balcony.

PHOTO BY LARRY WEILL

134

ATTRACTIONS OF LEWIS COUNTY

THE INTERNATIONAL MAPLE SYRUP MUSEUM CENTER

Maple. What American (or Canadian, or human being) doesn't love the taste of maple or maple syrup, especially when poured liberally over the top of a hot stack of freshly griddled pancakes? Almost no one, we would surmise.

Maple syrup is the one and only purpose for the existence of the International Maple Syrup Museum Center, located in the village of Croghan, New York. Here you will find everything that is maple, spread out over three floors of this brick-faced institution.

Front edifice of the International Maple Syrup Museum Center in Croghan.
PHOTO BY LARRY WEILL

On the day of my tour, Mr. John Altmire (the museum administrator) made a special trip to the facility to open it up for my visit. The museum is normally closed on Tuesdays, but Altmire was gracious enough to open its doors for me.

"The museum was opened in 1979, but was located in the town of Beaver Falls, New York," said Altmire. "It was moved to Croghan in 1980 following the donation of this building by Robert and Florence Lamb. The building used to be a Catholic school. It's really taken off since then, and we're very pleased with the growth of the museum."

The museum is dedicated to the goals of "preserving and promoting the industry in the heart of the biggest syrup-producing region in the United States." The museum now receives over 400 visitors per year, which has been increasing as the facility adds new functions onto its annual schedule. "We operate two 'maple syrup weekends' every year in the month of March," said Altmire. "We also do an annual ice cream social in the month of July, which is very popular and well-attended."

The people who operate the International Maple Syrup Museum Center are very passionate about what they do. The three floors of exhibits, which include rooms full of tools, evaporators, collection devices, and even snowshoes for "making the rounds," are extremely well organized and displayed with pride. This includes the International Maple Hall of Fame, located on the upper floor of the facility. This is, simply put, a shrine to those who have made extraordinary contributions to the industry and art of maple syrup. It is administered by the North American Maple Syrup Council and is beautifully presented in a special room of its own.

When asked about the difference between this museum and a similar facility in Vermont, Altmire is quick to point out that the museum in Croghan is operated as a not-for-profit organization.

The address is 9748 Main Street, Croghan, New York. The museum operates on limited hours and is closed on Tuesdays and Sundays (as of the time of this writing). Hours are Monday through Saturday, 11 a.m.–4 p.m. Contact the museum directly at 315-346-1107 to ask about current hours, or visit the website at www.maplemuseumcentre.org for additional details.

Tools of the maple trade on display in the museum's lower level.

PHOTO BY LARRY WEILL

LAKE BONAPARTE: FRENCH ROYALTY IN THE ADIRONDACKS

Of all things you would *not* expect to see in the Adirondacks, one of them would be a reference to a French emperor and military leader such as Napoleon Bonaparte. Napoleon, emperor of France from 1804 to 1814 and instigator of the Napoleonic Wars across Europe, played a major role in the history of Europe for over a decade. But he also had family ties that extended across the Atlantic and into our own Adirondack Park.

Sign on access road to Lake Bonaparte.
PHOTO BY LARRY WEILL

Napoleon's brother, Joseph, was born one year before him. He was known for being less ambitious and daring than his conquering sibling. Joseph became a lawyer and a diplomat, and Napoleon later installed him as king of Naples and Sicily. He also made him the king of Spain, a title he held for five years, from 1808 to 1813, until his brother's defeat at the Battle of Nations in 1813 and subsequent abdication of the French throne the following year.

In 1815, following the defeat and exile of Napoleon, Joseph went incognito and traveled onboard the *Commerce* to the United States. He carried a portion of his "box of jewels" with him, enough to support his lavish lifestyle and also purchase a large estate on the banks of the Delaware River in Bordentown, NJ. There he spared no expense to furnish and decorate his expansive home and grounds with all the luxury to which he was accustomed. He was known for entertaining in grand style, as well as for maintaining a massive library that at the time was the largest in the United States.

A few years after establishing his estate at Bordentown, Joseph purchased a large tract of land in upstate New York on the shores of what was then known as Lake Diana. There he established a hunting lodge and also built a sizable wooden residence about 8 miles away, in Natural Bridge, New York. Lake Diana was later renamed Lake Bonaparte, which is its current appellation.

It is not known how much time Joseph Bonaparte actually spent in his upstate residences. Some references state that he made only a handful of visits to these distant rural locations, and no evidence of them remains today.

Joseph traveled between the United States and Europe numerous times in the 1820s and 1830s, his freedom to travel being somewhat restored following his brother's death in 1821. His last visit to the United States was in 1839, after

View across Lake Bonaparte to the inspiring cliffs.
PHOTO BY LARRY WEILL

Remains of Joseph Bonaparte's house in Natural Bridge.
PUBLIC DOMAIN

which he returned to Europe (England) for the final time. A series of strokes that he suffered between 1840 and 1843 curtailed all future travel, and he passed away in Italy on July 24, 1844.

There are no traces of Joseph's residences on Lake Bonaparte or in Natural Bridge still standing, although there are descendants of the Bonaparte family still living in the United States.

TRAIN TRACKS FROM THE PAST

With so many train enthusiasts in this country, it's no surprise that there are a *lot* of museums that specialize in this mode of transportation. A quick online search located 154 such institutions with a wide variety of specializations, including everything from regional railway lines to miniature model trains. Lewis County has its own such museum, which is located in an old train depot in the town of Croghan.

It's not someplace you'd immediately recognize as a museum, or even as a train depot, although the tracks that run by the front of the building probably reveal some of its original pedigree. However, all that disappears once you walk in the front door. It is crammed, literally floor to ceiling, with everything rail related.

My tour guide through this transportation mecca was Laurie Halliday, historian of Croghan, New York. She described the events that led up to the purchase of the Croghan Depot of the Lowville-Beaver River Railway (L&BRR) and how it came to be used as a museum building.

Railway Historical Society of Northern New York in Croghan.
PHOTO BY LARRY WEILL

Display case in Railway Historical Society museum filled with various kinds of railroad lamps and lighting fixtures.
PHOTO BY LARRY WEILL

The railway that passes by the museum was first proposed in 1903. It was a "short-line" railroad that covered the 10.9 miles between Lowville and Croghan. Its purpose was to transport products from local commerce, farming, lumber, and the paper industry across the area. Construction started within a year, with full operations underway by January 1906.

The original business activity of the Lowville and Beaver River Railroad extended well into the 1930s. But then the increasing use of trucks to transport cargo across the region cut into its business, until it was finally abandoned in 1938. It was later acquired for historical interest and the potential for limited commercial use.

Today, the museum (which is built into the train depot) is operated by the Railway Historical Society of Northern New York. The museum is staffed and operated by volunteers and train enthusiasts, who would love to see the original engine (which requires repairs) operate once again.

To find the museum, take NY Route 12 North to the town of Lowville. Continue through Lowville to NY Route 812. Turn right onto Route 812, then take it to the town of Croghan. In the middle of town, a set of railroad tracks crosses the street. The museum is on the right side of the road.

The street address is 9784 State Route 812, Croghan, New York. You can visit the website at http://www.newyorktrains.com/, or call the museum at 315-346-6848. Check online before visiting, as hours are limited and are subject to change.

EARLY RELIGION IN THE ADIRONDACKS

Belfort, an early "settlement" within the town of Croghan, is home to a unique part of Adirondack history. Standing alone in a quiet clearing on Belfort Road is the Saint Vincent de Paul's Catholic Church. Built over 175 years ago, it is the oldest surviving Catholic church between the St. Lawrence Seaway and the Mohawk River.

Side view of Saint Vincent de Paul's Catholic Church in Belfort.
PHOTO BY LARRY WEILL

The church has none of the majestic grandeur of the historic Catholic churches in Europe, or even in major US cities. It is a one-story building completely made of wood. A close inspection reveals peeling paint, chipped panels, and aging window frames and doors. Yet the church maintains a certain ageless dignity that proclaims its long-standing religious heritage in this tiny community.

The church was built between 1843 and 1844 under the direction of LeRay De Chaumont (not to be confused with Jacques-Donatien LeRay de Chaumont, a father of the American Revolution). It is surrounded by two acres of land that serve primarily as a cemetery for those who lived in the settlement in previous centuries. One of the earliest gravestones in the plot is that of Jaques Bugnon. His stone notes that he was 47 years of age at death, but no actual dates are recorded.

Many of the other stones in the cemetery are broken or in need of repair, and the centuries of harsh climate have rendered some of the inscriptions illegible. Yet there are a number of stones that are more contemporary, with local residents marking some of these headstones with flags to commemorate their military service.

The bell in the church steeple was donated by a local group in 1885, and their names appear engraved on the bell's surface. It remains in place today.

Gravestones in the cemetery outside the church.
PHOTO BY LARRY WEILL

The church was originally part of the Diocese of Albany, although it was reassigned to the Diocese of Ogdensburg in 1872. It continues to operate on a limited basis under the leadership of Pastor Donald Manfred.

To find the church, follow NY Route 812 north from Croghan, then turn right onto Belfort Road. The church is at the intersection of Belfort Road and Erie Canal Road (on the right).

Sign on front of Saint Vincent de Paul's Catholic Church.
PHOTO BY LARRY WEILL

VERONICA'S ROADSIDE ART

The great artist Pablo Picasso once said, "Every child is an artist. The problem is how to remain an artist once he grows up." In the case of Veronica Terrillion, the reverse is apparently true. A truly remarkable woman without formal training got her start later in life and created something remarkable.

Veronica Terrillion was born around 1908, as best we can determine, and lived most of her life in the rural areas of Lewis County. She was a wonderful woman, friendly and outgoing, and very much devoted to religion. She loved people and engaging in conversation, which led her to a hobby that would literally bring thousands to her door.

Veronica was always a bit of an artist and became personally involved in the selection of timber for her family home. "She cut her own cedar trees for the construction of the house that you see today," said Justin Terrillion, her grandson, who lives in that very same house today. "She picked up a lot from her Uncle George, who was a master stone mason, but she also learned a lot of it on her own."

Although Veronica didn't get started in her artistic endeavors until her late forties, she quickly made up for lost time and was prolific. She began turning out her trademark statues with amazing speed, focusing on animals as well

Statues of zebras and other favorite animals displayed on the Terrillion property in Croghan.
Photo by Larry Weill

142

as religious themes. "She loved creating works of art that bore out her religious faith," said her grandson. "So many people used to stop by and talk to her about her works; she had 20–30 guest books filled with people who stopped by to chat. Rather than the art itself, we have come to the realization that the real attraction was Veronica herself."

Terrillion became well known both inside and outside her community. The museum known as TAUNY (Traditional Arts in Upstate New York) Center in Canton, New York, owns and displays several of Veronica's works as part of its permanent collection, thanks to the generosity of Justin Terrillion and his family. The curator of this facility was a longtime friend of the artist.

Veronica Terrillion passed away in 2004, at the age of 96. She was active in the arts until quite late in life (about age 90), although her deteriorating physical condition limited her activities in later years. Her grandson stated that many of the statues have begun to crumble with age, although quite a few still exist in excellent condition. Her works can be observed at the family home on NY Route 812 in Croghan and can be viewed and appreciated from the side of the road. Please note, however, that all the works on display are on private property, so please respect the privacy of the current residents. But do feel free to stop and take photographs. Veronica most certainly would have approved!

The address is 11051 State Route 812, Croghan, New York. You can view everything from the roadside. To see more call 315-386-4289 for an appointment.

Religious-themed statue, viewed over the small pond on the Terrillion property.
PHOTO BY LARRY WEILL

WHERE'S THE BEEF? NEW YORK STATE'S LARGEST COW

"Lady Lewinda Milkzalot" standing outside the Lowville Producers Cheese Store.
PHOTO BY LARRY WEILL

Lowville Producers Cheese Store.
PHOTO BY LARRY WEILL

How many hamburgers could you get from a cow that is approximately 10 feet tall and about 12 feet long? Or, more appropriately, how many gallons of milk could you collect from it every day?

These questions are irrelevant, as this massive animal is a bit on the artificial side. With its enormous stature, "Lady Lewinda Milkzalot" has the distinct honor of being the largest cow in the state of New York, even if it has never emitted a single "moo" in its entire existence.

The huge cow statue has become an icon of the Lowville Producers Cheese Store, which is a cooperative business that brings together about 165 dairy farmers across the area between the lower Adirondacks and the Tug Hill Plateau. It has been in operation since 1936, and the proud history of the operation is on display inside the well-stocked store.

A few of the co-op business partners discussed the cow and mentioned that it had been acquired for the property sometime around 2005–2006. "It draws a lot of families here every year, I wish I had a dollar for every person who has stopped to photograph Lady Lewinda," said one of the co-op members.

While the cow has the ability to make motorists stop, it's the cheese store that is responsible for people sticking around to shop. It is one of those places that just grabs your attention and holds onto it, as there is so much to see inside. "We have over 75 different varieties of cheese inside this store," said Lynn Cole, the store manager. "No matter what you want, chances are pretty good that we have a cheese type to match your taste."

Cheeses run the gamut from the common varieties such as American, cheddar, and Monterey Jack to "killer dill," mushroom leek, and strawberry chardonnay. Many of them are on display in the shop and are available for purchase.

Samples of various varieties are also available in the shop, so you can try before you buy.

The store also offers a wide variety of noncheese products, including canned and pickled vegetables, candy, maple products (including syrup, cream, and candy), honey, and the famous Croghan bologna.

Both the cow and the store can be found at 7396 Utica Boulevard, Lowville, New York. The phone number is 315-376-3921, or visit the website at https://

Lynn Cole, manager of Lowville Producers Cheese Store, with a sample gift box containing co-op products.
PHOTO BY LARRY WEILL

www.GotGoodCheese.com. The store is open Monday through Saturday from 8:00 a.m.–5:00 p.m.

VALLEY BROOK DRIVE-IN (RETRO 1950s)

When we think back on the weekends of the 1950s and 1960s (for those of us who remember those days), our minds often take us to places that no longer exist. One of those early pleasures was the drive-in movie, which was simply a large outdoor movie screen with rows of car speakers. You'd grab your friends and pile into whatever wheels you had for a night in front of the silver screen, usually with food in hand from the facility's snack bar.

The Valley Brook Drive-in is one of those places, one of only a handful of drive-ins still in existence. "Believe it or not, there are only about 300 drive-ins still in operation in the United States," said Mike Dekin, owner and operator of the Valley Brook facility. "There are 31 or 32 left in the State of New York, although quite a few states don't have a single one."

Dekin's story is a fascinating tale of perseverance and determination. The theater was opened by his grandparents in 1952, and he became involved with it while still in high school. "In 1983, the theater wasn't going to open at all," said Dekin. "Then my grandmother asked me if I could run the place. She gave me a couple weeks' instruction on how to prepare the film in the cameras and how to run the other equipment needed to keep the facility in operation. I gradually got better and better at doing things, so here I am today, still open for business. We've gone through a lot in those years, but we've managed to keep it going."

Entrance to the Valley Brook Drive-in in Lyons Falls.

PHOTO BY LARRY WEILL

The main projection screen of the Valley Brook Drive-in.

PHOTO BY LARRY WEILL

Like most drive-in theaters, the Valley Brook is not open year-round. The schedule changes a bit from year to year, but it closes for the winter and usually opens again in the middle of May. Most of the customers are either locals or people who are visiting the area for a few weeks.

"Lewis County only has about 27,000 residents, and many of those are farmers who work long hours," said Dekin. "They often look for cheap entertainment, which is what we offer. Oneida County lost their drive-in, so we get some of their residents visiting us as well. It's a night out under the stars with good food and good movies for the family."

Along with great movies, the Valley Brook offers a snack bar that serves up hamburgers, hot dogs, French fries, popcorn, and more.

The facility has also kept up with the times and offers its "sound system" via an FM radio station. "We used to have about 400 car speakers that people mounted in their car windows," said Dekin. "But we ended up spending the entire week fixing the things, which kept breaking with age. So now we've got the radio station, which provides a much better sound."

Mike runs the theater on weekends (Friday through Sunday) as a part-time gig and works for the state the rest of the week. He manages to keep the entire operation running with the help of a few part-time helpers, which is an amazing accomplishment in today's environment. There are two movies every night, which start once it is dark enough to show on the big screen. The "main event" film usually runs for about two weeks, while the second film changes more frequently.

The address is 6610 Burdicks Crossing Road, Lyons Falls, New York. To view the theater's film schedule, check out its Facebook page at https://www.facebook.com/ValleyBrookDriveInTheater/.

ATTRACTIONS OF JEFFERSON COUNTY

THE BENTON-BONAPARTE HOUSE, OXBOW, NEW YORK

The town of Oxbow, New York, is located in Jefferson County, none of which is contained inside the boundaries of the Adirondack Park. However, because of this story's inextricable link to Joseph Bonaparte, Napoleon's brother, it is hereby included in this accounting of Adirondack lore.

Caroline was the illegitimate daughter of Joseph Bonaparte, who had traveled to the United States in 1815, following his brother's defeat at the hands of the Duke of Wellington at Waterloo. Once in the United States, Joseph purchased properties and established himself in several locations, including Philadelphia, Pennsylvania, and Bordentown, New Jersey. He also acquired a large property in Upstate New York that contained a body of water he renamed Lake Diana. That body of water has since been named Lake Bonaparte, in honor of the European family of conquerors.

Home of Caroline Bonaparte in Oxbow.
PHOTO BY LARRY WEILL

Sign in front of the Benton-Bonaparte House.
PHOTO BY LARRY WEILL

The house, which is prominently labeled "The Benton-Bonaparte House," was built between 1816 and 1819 by Dr. Abner Benton. Benton's son, Zebulon Benton, later married Caroline. They established themselves in this residence and lived there until the late 1890s (the exact year is not known to historians).

Today this house is privately owned by Ms. Jeanne Gincel, who graciously led the author on a tour of the building and explained its current configuration compared to its original structure. Most of the original house is still intact, although some rooms have been modified as their use has changed over the years.

There have also been stories about a tunnel in the basement that was connected to other buildings as part of the Underground Railroad. Ms. Gincel was quick to explain that these tunnels are long since gone, having fallen victim to the ravages of time.

"From the stories that have been passed down, the tunnel caved in long ago. Supposedly, it was connected to a barn that was located closer to the river. Escaped slaves could travel through the tunnel and prepare to be smuggled onto boats for the ride that would take them closer to Canada and freedom," Gincel said. "The tunnel was originally very small and narrow, and the escapees had to crawl through its passage in order to get through to the other side. However, even the entrance to what was the tunnel has been bricked over, and nothing is left of the tunnel itself."

Jeanne Gincel is also the head of the Oxbow Historical Society and escorted the author on a tour of the Oxbow Museum,

Grave of Caroline Benton-Bonaparte in Oxbow.
PHOTO BY LARRY WEILL

which is situated next to the small cemetery in which Caroline is buried. The Oxbow Historical Society/Museum is located on Church Street (no number) in Oxbow, New York.

THE OTHER STATUE OF LIBERTY

Almost everyone knows the location of the Statue of Liberty. About 3.5 million people visit the colossal figure on Liberty Island every year, and even more get turned away due to the maximum number of visitors permitted. On some days, as many as 15,000 sightseers attempt to reach the island to pay their respects.

A lesser-known fact is that there are other copies of this statue on display in various parts of the world, including two smaller versions in Paris, France. However, one even shorter version of Miss Liberty graces the town of Philadelphia, New York, in Jefferson County.

It's not something that is well known, even within the town itself. (The author asked a local resident encountered on the sidewalk in town, and that person did not know where to find it.) You almost have to know where to look, as it is located between a service station and a car wash. But it is there on display, compliments of the proud people at Philly Fuels, Inc.

Philly Fuels, Inc., is a fuel company that sells and distributes various kinds of fuel (including gasoline, fuel oil, heating oil, diesel, and wooden pellets) over a wide area. The company opened its doors in 1982 under the ownership of Elmer and Susan Hoover, and they've never looked back. Today they've grown their business many times over and the entire family has become involved.

One thing that is not immediately obvious is the pride and patriotism of this local family, although that becomes instantly visible with one stroll past their memorial plot. It is truly a sight to see.

Susan Hoover, business owner, says that the statue itself came from a

Statue of Liberty replica on display in Philadelphia.
PHOTO BY LARRY WEILL

store in New York City in 2012 and was brought up to Philadelphia in the back of a pickup truck. "We filled the bed of the truck with sawdust to protect it from harm," she said. "The statue actually appeared in an episode of *Law & Order*, so it has an interesting history."

It was interesting to learn that the Hoover family has no actual ties to the US military, even though their patriotism is on display every day. "We are an extremely patriotic family," said Britney Hoover, daughter of the owner. "Each one of our fuel delivery trucks carries an American flag, and our property around the station here is circled with 'blue stripe' American flags in the summer."

The duplicate Statue of Liberty on display at Philly Fuels, Inc., is about 18 to 20 feet tall, including the base. By comparison, the real version in New York harbor is 305 feet tall, which also includes the base. The Hoover family had the concrete base crafted to resemble the "real McCoy" in almost every aspect. It looks like the real deal.

To see the statue in Philadelphia, go to 5 N US Route 11, Philadelphia. If you need to contact the owners by phone, their number is (315) 642-5562. They also operate a lovely store inside the Philly fuels building where you can get everything from coffee to dog biscuits. They would love to see you!

AREA 51—IN NEW YORK STATE!

Sign at the Vortex in Thompson Park, Watertown.

Photo by Larry Weill

Most of the attractions listed in this book are located inside of the Adirondack Blue Line. Those that are not are found in counties that are at least partially inside the park. However, there is one site in Watertown's Thompson Park (Jefferson County) that has links to other galaxies!

The sign announcing the presence of the supernatural site is located on the hill that is home to the Watertown Zoo. Located at 1 Thompson Park, Watertown, New York, this hilltop park has entrances off the Park Circle, Gotham Street, and Franklin Street. The phone number is 315-785-7775. The entrance to "the Vortex" is not inside the zoo itself. Instead, it is located on an exercise trail near the northern boundary of Thompson Park, a 366-acre plot of land that has been open since 1930. (There are several varying dates found online regarding its acquisition and development, starting with 1899.)

Rumors have abounded over the years that there is a "vortex" inside Thompson Park that has the ability to transport people to other locations inside the park, and even to alter the passage of time. Reports of people seeking the entrance to the Vortex range from feeling dizzy, to weak, to extremely disoriented. Other people describe being transported to other locations within the park and onto trails where they had not hiked on their own. Some accounts have even mentioned park users who have vanished and not reappeared at all, although these stories are few and far between. Also, the entrance to the Vortex has a reputation for changing locations throughout the park.

To find the Vortex sign, continue past the zoo entrance (to the right of the gate) and follow the black outside fence to the right a few hundred yards. It will lead to the fitness trail, which is a loop containing a number of fitness stops (i.e., metal bars used for doing sit-ups, chin-ups, and other exercises). The Vortex sign is found opposite the "Inclined Body Curl" station.

Sign showing the path to the Charles R. Hyde Memorial Fitness Trail, where the Vortex sign is found.

Photo by Larry Weill

If you would like to visit the Vortex at Thompson Park, you can gain entry off Gotham Street, Academy Street, or Franklin Street in Watertown. The park is open from 7:00 a.m. through 9:00 p.m. year-round, and entrance is free to the public.

If you are worried about disappearing into the Vortex, you may want to consider taking a friend. The author (who does not believe in supernatural phenomena like this) was unaccompanied. Nothing happened to him, until suddenly he

CROWS ON THE HIGHWAY!

Interstate 81 is a major highway in upstate New York that runs from the Pennsylvania state line to the Canadian border. Driving those 183 miles of monotonous pavement can lull your senses until you are thoroughly bored to tears, focused only on the long stretch of road between you and the next exit. However, there is one short section of road on which you should be ready to cast a glance out your passenger-side window.

The site of interest is located on I-81 South, about 3 miles after the highway crosses NY Route 12. There, in an open field, are three giant crow sculptures created by the late artist Will Salisbury. Salisbury fashioned the crows out of sheet metal, which has been painted "crow black." They stand about 8 to 10 feet tall and are uniquely lifelike in their appearance. If viewed at a distance, they could be confused with the real thing, which has undoubtedly happened over the years.

Will Salisbury (1949–2022) was a beloved resident of the Thousand Islands region who was a fixture in his community for half his lifetime. Over the years he concentrated his attention and talents on art, philosophy, teaching, and much more. He was a prolific sculptor who worked in a great variety of media, including steel, copper, stone, wood, and ceramics. His works, which often focused on subjects of social importance, can be found in museums, art centers, and public gathering places across the region.

The series of crow sculptures on I-81 is perhaps one of Salisbury's best-known works of art, simply due to its position of prominence along the major thoroughfare. However,

Three crow sculptures by Will Salisbury in Oman.

please be cautioned: Stopping on the shoulder of the highway is not safe or legal and can lead to a traffic ticket (or worse). The best views of these sculptures are for the *passenger* in your car looking out the right-side window.

There are also a number of sculptures situated in a field across the street from Salisbury's studio, on County Road 13 in the town of LaFargeville. These works of art run the gamut from stone monoliths to welded conglomerations of bicycles and bed frames. Many of the subjects represented in the artworks seem to "speak" to the viewer with genuine emotion and passion.

Thought-provoking stone sculpture across the street from Will Salisbury's workshop.
PHOTO BY LARRY WEILL

"Some of the sculptures on the other side of the road were 'prototypes' of Salisbury's later works," said Nolan Irvine, Salisbury's nephew. "The stone sculpture that sits next to the road was actually a work by Carmen D'Avino, another accomplished artist from Hammond, New York. He passed away before the work was completed, so my uncle and another artist completed the piece."

The workshop on the property is open to the public whenever Nolan or his parents (who now live in the residence on the property) are around. "You can purchase any of my uncle's sculptures, carvings, or sketchings" said Irvine. "You are also welcome to park

Welded bike frames appear to be whirling in space in this unusual piece of sculpture.
PHOTO BY LARRY WEILL

in front of the studio building and walk up the path to see the crow sculptures."

The address for the studio is 40812 County Road 13, LaFargeville, New York. The path to the crow sculptures is up a steep hill to the right of the studio.

ATTRACTIONS OF ESSEX COUNTY

THE NORTH POLE (INSIDE SANTA'S WORKSHOP)

Visiting Santa's Workshop in Wilmington, New York, is like taking a step back in time, perhaps 70 years. Most of it hasn't changed a bit in all those decades, a fact not lost on those who run the place.

"Santa's Workshop is known for that, and we're proud of our reputation," said Helen Coolidge, operations manager of the popular attraction. "Most of the buildings and rides and shows are original, and have been in place since we opened in 1949. Many people don't realize this, but we're actually the oldest theme park in the United States. But some things have changed. We used to have live animals, including goats, walking around the grounds, but they're not there anymore."

Santa's Workshop has become such an iconic part of Adirondack nostalgia that many people come back year after year, bringing their children and then their grandchildren to visit. They tend to gravitate to some of those original rides, such as the train and the roller coaster.

The North Pole inside Santa's Workshop in Wilmington.
PHOTO BY LARRY WEILL

Children's Ferris wheel at Santa's Workshop.
PHOTO BY LARRY WEILL

Coolidge says that most visitors come from New York State and surrounding areas, although "we do get visitors from all across the United States, plus some from Canada." She estimates that they average about 350 visitors each day, although that number swells to over 1,000 a day during the winter months.

"We're open every day from the last weekend in June until Labor Day, and remain open on weekends until Columbus Day," said Coolidge. "But then we re-open in November, before Thanksgiving, and stay open on weekends through Christmas. Those are some of our busiest days of the year."

When asked about the North Pole itself, the tall, frozen pole sticking up out of the ground for all to touch, Coolidge says that "yes, it does draw a lot of attention. A lot of people walk up and put their hand upon it without realizing that it's really frozen." To date, however, no one can remember anyone ever getting their tongue stuck to the pole.

The address is 324 Whiteface Memorial Highway, Wilmington, New York. People interested in visiting the North Pole at Santa's Workshop can call 518-946-2211, or visit www.northpoleny.com for details.

FRONTIER TOWN GHOST VILLAGE (SCHROON LAKE)

Visiting the Adirondacks conjures up thoughts of majestic mountains, fishing in trout-laden streams, and camping in the wilderness. One thing that does *not* come to mind is a cowboy riding a bucking bull or the cavalry riding down the street en route to the frontier.

Yet that is exactly what visitors to Frontier Town got at the now-defunct theme park, located right off Interstate 87 in the town of Schroon Lake. The

Sign for Frontier Town, now a ghost village in Schroon Lake.
PHOTO BY LARRY WEILL

park opened its gates to the public in 1952 and succeeded in attracting crowds for several decades. The grounds included many western-themed attractions and shows, including various cowboy-related activities, a stagecoach ride, Native American events, and (of course) a plethora of stores where tourists could spend their hard-earned dollars.

Several factors led to the decline of attendance at this Adirondack slice of the West, including the emergence of larger and more extravagant parks across the country, including the Disney mega-parks in Florida and others.

The park closed for good in 1998 and has stood since that time as an abandoned and rotting reminder of what used to be. The large Frontier Town sign still stands alongside the road at the entrance to the front parking lot (previous photo). Beyond that, a number of buildings still remain, although none are in good condition, and many are collapsing in place.

Visitors to this site should know that they can still walk around and view many of the original buildings, but they should not consider entering any structure that has not been properly maintained (none have). As in any "ghost town" or abandoned site, the walls and ceilings are unstable and may collapse at any time. Additionally, many of the wooden boardwalks throughout the site have decayed to the point where rusty nails are found protruding from the boards, making it extremely dangerous to attempt to walk on them.

If you plan to view the remains of this ghost village, you had better make it quick, as several of the buildings have already been torn down for safety reasons

Rear view of main front building with deteriorating bridge.
Photo by Larry Weill

and new development. The state is supposedly moving ahead with plans for a campground, hiking and horseback riding trails, and more.

To visit, follow the Adirondack Northway (I-87) north to US Route 9 and Frontier Town Road (exit 29 on the Northway) in the town of Schroon Lake. Hike at your own risk.

THE BLAST FURNACE AND GHOST VILLAGE AT TAHAWUS

Even for a region that is filled with dozens of "ghost villages," the deserted settlement at Tahawus stands alone. The village got its start in 1826, when two men, Archibald McIntyre and David Henderson, attempted to start an iron mining and smelting facility in the region just south of the High Peaks Tahawus Preserve, sometimes referred to as Upper Works.

The village was originally called McIntyre, in honor of Archibald McIntyre, but has gone through multiple appellations, including Adirondac (spelled without the final "k") and Tahawus. Unfortunately for the two major stakeholders, the iron works met its demise after facing a number of crises, including McIntyre's death and a major flood.

The mining operation also faced numerous logistical problems, including the presence of a stubborn impurity in the ore and the eventual shortage of locally sourced fuel to run the blast furnace. (One of the more ironic sides to this history was the discovery of the identity of the impurity, which turned out to be

Enormous blast furnace at Tahawus, whose size can be appreciated by looking at the scale of the author, standing inside the lower masonry arch.
PHOTO BY LARRY WEILL

158

titanium, element number 22 on the Periodic Chart. Immensely strong and of vital importance to the defense industry, it nonetheless rendered the iron ore extremely difficult to refine.)

The massive blast furnace, which was constructed from 1849 to 1853, was operated for only a few short years, commencing in 1854 and ending in 1855. Although the site was used for other purposes in later years, the final death knell of the iron works was sounded by the flooding in 1857. The remains of the industrial equipment used in the smelting process were left behind, rusting in nearby pits and holding grounds.

Even though the site is so dominated by the presence of the monstrous furnace, many other historic structures and ruins remain. The most significant of these buildings, and the only one being actively maintained, is the MacNaughton Cottage (otherwise called the McMartin House), which was constructed in 1834. This house gained notoriety when Vice President Teddy Roosevelt stayed there while climbing Mount Marcy in September 1901. He left this residence on his now-fabled, frantic "midnight ride" to North Creek, where he was sworn in as the 26th president of the United States.

One of many decaying structures in the woods at Upper Works.
PHOTO BY LARRY WEILL

New York State has worked to improve the Tahawus site at Upper Works over the years and has reportedly knocked down some of the dangerously decayed and leaning structures interspersed throughout the woods. If you visit the area today, you are invited to learn from the interpretational trails and signs placed among the ruins and around the blast furnace. However, remain clear of any unimproved or unrestored buildings, which may easily collapse at any time.

The route to Upper Works and the blast furnace departs from NY Route 28N where NY Route

MacNaughton Cottage, which housed Teddy Roosevelt until the day he was sworn in as president.
PHOTO BY LARRY WEILL

25 turns north, also called Blue Ridge Road, before turning into Tahawus Road. The total distance to the blast furnace is approximately 12 miles from the Route 28N turnoff. Consult local maps for more detailed guidance.

BREWERY WITH A CURIOUS LINK TO THE COLD WAR

Since this travel guide is primarily a reference to the unusual and historic attractions of the Adirondacks, it might seem out of place that a brewery is listed here. Yet because of another historic site that is also included in this volume, this establishment is entirely relevant.

Sign in front of Big Slide Brewery & Public House outside Lake Placid.

PHOTO BY LARRY WEILL

Big Slide Brewery sits on NY Route 73 (Cascade Road) on the south side of Lake Placid. Although it has only been open since 2015, it is connected to another local establishment (the Lake Placid Pub & Brewery), which opened its doors in 1996. Chris Ericson, who owns and operates both of these brew pubs, has crafted unique food, drink, and atmosphere in each of his locations, and the Lake Placid crowd (as well as the tourists) have taken notice.

Ericson is also a superb judge of brewing talent, as evidenced by the hiring of Kevin Litchfield as his director of brewing operations in 1999. Litchfield spoke passionately about getting into the brewing business and learning his trade. "Back when I was getting into it, you pretty much had to find an apprenticeship somewhere and learn by experience," said Litchfield. "Nowadays, there are college programs that offer a formal education that is much more structured. But I like what I do, and I've never regretted learning on-the-job, as I did back then."

Tanks for brewing beer in Big Slide Brewery.

PHOTO BY LARRY WEILL

Litchfield's background has included numerous other activities, perhaps none more important than his stint as the cross-country coach at Paul Smith's College in 2004. It was there that he met Dan Burke, the owner of Atlas Hoofed It Farm (see "Attractions of Franklin County"). While Litchfield was coaching the cross-country team, Burke was employed as the school's women's soccer coach. The two developed a friendship, and Dan offered up the possibility of allowing Big Slide Brewery to age beers in the depths of the Atlas missile silo, located on his hilltop farm.

"We talked about the idea, but nothing really came of it," said Litchfield. "We sort of forgot about it until I called Dan back about 10 years later and asked if his offer was still good. He said yes, and the rest is history."

Once the stout was produced, the real work got started, as they carried the many kegs of brew down the dark, steep stairs into the concrete bunkers. These rooms, located 25 feet below the surface, remain at a constant 55 degrees Fahrenheit year-round, offering a perfect climate for the aging process. The resulting beer, Russian Imperial Stout, was a resounding success and sold out in the brewery within a matter of weeks.

Litchfield noted that, although there are no immediate plans to use the Cold War–era missile silo for aging additional beers soon, they have not ruled out such activity in the future. For now, you can enjoy their superb products by stopping by the Big Slide Brewery, located at 5686 Cascade Road, Lake Placid, New York, or visit https://www.bigslidebrewery.com/.

WHERE TEDDY ROOSEVELT BECAME PRESIDENT

Teddy Roosevelt, our nation's twenty-sixth president, was serving as William McKinley's vice president when McKinley was shot by an anarchist at the Pan American Exposition in Buffalo, New York, on September 6, 1901. Roosevelt was on Lake Champlain at the time of the shooting but immediately traveled to Buffalo to be with McKinley following the assassination attempt.

By September 10, McKinley's condition had improved to the point where Roosevelt felt his presence was no longer required. He departed for the Tahawus Club in the Adirondacks, which he used as a jumping-off point for a climb of Mount Marcy, the state's tallest peak.

President Theodore "Teddy" Roosevelt.

While Roosevelt was engaged in his ascent, McKinley's health took a sharp turn for the worse, and a guide was dispatched on September 13 to find Roosevelt and inform him of the circumstances. Roosevelt immediately returned to the club and prepared to return to Buffalo the next day. However, around midnight he grew impatient and decided to begin the journey immediately.

Roosevelt was never known for being overcautious, and on this fateful evening he certainly lived up to his reputation. Traveling over rough, darkened roads with a series of drivers pulling horse-drawn carriages, Roosevelt made the seven-hour trip to the North Creek train station in under five hours. The distance of the trip is estimated at no less than 35 miles. Several historians have noted that it was a wonder we didn't lose two presidents that night.

Roosevelt's frantic midnight ride has been commemorated many times over the years, but perhaps the first to do so was Harry Radford. Radford was many things to many people: a student, a writer and editor, a photographer, an explorer, a hunter, and later an instigator whose quick temper and ill-advised aggression led to his demise at the hands of some Inuit natives on Hudson Bay.

It was Radford who, in 1908, erected a memorial to Roosevelt on the side of NY Route 28N east of Newcomb, New York. The plaque was replaced in 2014, as

Plaque commemorating the spot through which Teddy Roosevelt passed when McKinley died and Roosevelt became president of the United States.

Photo by Larry Weill

the aging process and the extreme climate had caused it to separate from the boulder that supported it. The town of Newcomb appears to be dedicated to preserving the memorial and had a spare plaque produced in case the current one is ever stolen or damaged.

The memorial can be found by following Route 28N about 21 miles east of the Long Lake junction with NY Route 30 (in front of Hoss's Country Store), 3.0 miles beyond Newcomb, New York, and 1.2 miles east of the historic marker at Blueridge Road.

Full text of the plaque commemorating Teddy Roosevelt's midnight trip to North Creek.
PHOTO BY LARRY WEILL

HOW SWEET IT IS! THE SOUTH MEADOW MAPLE FARM

The Adirondacks are not generally known for having the world's most fertile soil; thus not a great many farms are seen as one drives along the park's roads. One thing that is found in abundance are trees, and a great many of those are maples. This has given rise to a large maple syrup business that provides income to many maple farmers across the region.

One of the more resourceful and successful of these is the team of Tony and Nancy Corwin, owners and operators of the South Meadow Maple Farm, located on the outskirts of Lake Placid. A hardy couple, they have resided at South Meadow Maple Farm for 31 years (since 1992).

"Making maple syrup was really more of a hobby than a business when we got started back in 1996," said Tony. "At the time, I didn't know it was going to turn into our major source of

Tony and Nancy Corwin, owners of South Meadow Maple Farm near Lake Placid, outside their store and evaporating facility.
PHOTO BY LARRY WEILL

The Corwins standing next to their steam-powered evaporator.
PHOTO BY LARRY WEILL

Some of the products found on the shelves of the store at South Meadow Maple Farm.
PHOTO BY LARRY WEILL

Clever license plate displayed inside the South Meadow Maple Farm store.
PHOTO BY LARRY WEILL

income. But then the ice storm of 1997 came along and many of the other maple producers had a difficult time getting a sap crop to work with that year. We were able to produce a large harvest and make our syrup when others couldn't, so we built a large list of clientele quite quickly."

To keep up with demand, Tony has tap lines running to about 10,000 trees, although not all are located on the farm's property. "We have about 75 acres of land on the farm, but we also lease some land and tap those trees to boost our yield," he said. The farm uses the tapped sap to churn out about 4,000 gallons of maple syrup every year.

South Meadow Maple Farm operates a wonderful store on the premises that offers a wide variety of products, including many that are not maple related. The store sells maple syrup, jams, jellies, spreads, pickled vegetables, and more. It is open to the public, and is completely self-serve.

In addition to the maple farm, the Corwins also own and operate a bed and breakfast that is open year-round. Seven attractively decorated rooms and suites are located inside the lodge. Prices are very reasonable and remain constant throughout the year. Children are welcome at the lodge, although pets are not permitted.

If you would like to stay at the South Meadow Maple Farm & Lodge, you can make reservations online at https://southmeadow.com/. You can also call the farm at 518-523-9369. If you just want to visit the store, it is located at 67 Sugarworks Way, Lake Placid, New York.

WINEMAKING IN THE ADIRONDACKS! HIGHLANDS VINEYARD

When the subject of winemaking and vineyards comes up, most people think about the Finger Lakes of New York or the Sonoma Valley in California. Many people don't realize that the Adirondacks are home to some superb vineyards where a unique variety of wines are produced.

Entrance to Highlands Vineyard in Keeseville.
PHOTO BY LARRY WEILL

One such facility is Highlands Vineyard, a *gorgeous* place nestled against the shoreline of Lake Champlain in Essex County. Everything about this place is amazing, from the views to the production facility to the people who run the winemaking process. It is unique in many ways in the Adirondack region.

Highlands Vineyard is a family-run business, with six family members all involved in every phase of the operations. Frank Campagna, a retired bank executive, served as my host during my visit. Also present were his wife (Kathleen), son and daughter-in-law (Ryan and Lindsey), and Lindsey's parents (Randy and Terry Ashline).

Inside the store and tasting rooms of Highlands Vineyard.
PHOTO BY LARRY WEILL

The story of the beginnings of Highlands is a fascinating combination of smart business sense with a love of nature and wine. The land on which the vineyard is planted became available in 2012. It was located behind the Ashlines' home and presented a wonderful view overlooking the lake. This gave them the idea of planting northern-sustainable grapes and entering the winemaking business.

"We had a lot of work to do before we ever got started planting grapes," said Frank. "The 12 acres of grapes you see growing here were all originally covered with trees. We bought some used equipment and got to work clearing the ground, which took a lot of time and effort."

Once the land was cleared, the entire family (aided by friends) got to work planting the grape vines. These included 12 different varieties, which were specially selected for their suitability to the local climate and weather.

"Unfortunately, some of the other vineyards in the region planted varieties grown in California, which aren't adapted to cold weather," said Frank. "So they may grow well for a couple years, but then one bad winter will kill their entire crop." The family credits the assistance they received from Cornell Cooperative Extension in selecting the appropriate varieties to plant on their property.

Highlands grows 12 varieties of grapes, including 7 red and 5 white. From these they produce a luscious array of seven specialty wines with seductive names such as Moonlight (a Sabrevois red wine aged in bourbon barrels) and Blush (Catawba and Brianna wines blended to produce a sweet rosé). The grapes run the gamut of dry to very sweet and fruity, which lend their characteristics to the variety of wine produced.

In addition to wine, Highlands Vineyard also produces other products, including maple syrup. "There are about 1,000 maple trees around the vineyard

View down the road at Highlands Vineyard to a hill leading to Lake Champlain.
PHOTO BY LARRY WEILL

that we tap every year," said Frank. "Some of the syrup is even used to add a hint of maple to our 'Maple' wine, which is a Louise Swenson dry white wine."

A view of the oak barrels inside the aging room.
PHOTO BY LARRY WEILL

Highlands Vineyard is unique as a business because it is so much more than a winemaking facility. "We are the only facility around which grows our own grapes, produces our own wines, and runs a tasting room along with an events venue," said Frank. "People come here to hold their weddings, corporate events, and more. Plus, we offer 'estate wines,' which means that they are produced from grapes grown on our own acres."

Even more astounding is the fact that the entire facility was built from timber that came from clearing their land and locally sourced granite. "Our entire family has been in on this," said Frank. "Our son and his father-in-law, Randy Ashline, built much of the store and tasting room building using wood from the site. It uses geothermal heating, so it saves fuel and is extremely efficient."

Likewise, the entire family is involved with producing the wine itself. "We bottled 3,500 bottles yesterday," Frank stated. "We worked from 7:00 a.m. until 7:00 p.m., and then we all sat down together for dinner."

The vineyard is a wonderful place to visit, and many people who have "discovered it" choose to return year after year. It is located at 1092 Highland Road, Keeseville, New York. The phone number is 518-836-5355,or visit www .highlandsvineyards.com.

NOTE OF CAUTION TO WINE ENTHUSIASTS

I'd like to issue a word of caution to wine enthusiasts looking to visit vineyards and wine-tasting rooms up and down the "Adirondack Wine Trail." Please make sure that you *call ahead to any vineyard or winery you hope to visit* while touring the trail. I personally started at some of the northernmost facilities, near Chazy, New York, and then headed south along the Wine Trail. The first four facilities I visited were no longer in operation.

Each location I visited was closed or simply gone, removed from the site for a variety of reasons. These reasons included lack of business, difficulties in producing a crop, or the health of the vineyard owners. (Someone once told me that the best way to "make a small fortune in the business of winemaking was to start with a *large* fortune!")

Please note that I am not suggesting that *all* the vineyards on this trail are gone. Some are actually thriving, producing some excellent wines and welcoming visitors to their facilities for tasting and purchasing their products. But I do recommend that you *call ahead* to ensure that your specific destinations are still in business and open to the public.

Enjoy!

THE COVERED BRIDGE IN JAY

One of the most romantic sights imaginable is a covered bridge spanning a cool, clear stream in a country setting. There is something so peaceful and so picturesque that people literally flock to these settings for photographs and events. Many a wedding has been conducted inside these charming remnants from the past, and they are celebrated wherever they may be.

For reasons unknown, people automatically think of Vermont as the home of the most covered bridges in the Northeast, but this is far from the truth. Many guides to the topic credit the state of Pennsylvania with having as many as 219

The covered bridge spanning the Ausable River in Jay.
PHOTO BY LARRY WEILL

of these historic structures. Ohio can claim 42 covered bridges, and many other states have between 5 and 20. The tally provided for the state of New York varies, but at least 7 bridges appear on all the lists compiled for the state.

Perhaps the longest and best-constructed bridge on this list is in the town of Jay, New York. It spans the beautiful Ausable River and is somewhere between 160 and 175 feet in length. (It shouldn't be that difficult to measure, but no one seems to take the time to bring along a tape measure to make the final determination.)

The Jay Covered Bridge is a historic structure for several reasons. First, it was built in 1857 by George Burt and is the only remaining wooden bridge in the Adirondacks that utilizes the "Howe Truss" method of construction. This technique, which was invented by William Howe in 1840, used upper and lower horizontal "chords" in conjunction with vertical beams and diagonal "bracings." These wooden beams (which were later augmented with iron rods) used tension and compression to mutually support one another in an impressively strong lattice. The Jay Covered Bridge is also the northernmost covered bridge left in the state of New York.

Looking across the Ausable River through one end of the Jay Covered Bridge.
Photo by Larry Weill

View of the unique "Howe Truss" construction beams inside the Jay Covered Bridge.
PHOTO BY LARRY WEILL

This bridge has been through a lot since its construction, having been damaged or destroyed on multiple occasions by weather, floods, and even motorized vehicles. (A truck fell through its floor in 1953.) The work to restore the bridge to its current, fully restored condition was completed in 2006. The new, modern bridge that carries traffic across the Ausable River is a short distance downstream from the covered bridge, which is now completely free of vehicular traffic.

To find the Jay Covered Bridge, follow NY Route 86 out of Lake Placid and through the village of Willington, New York. Route 86 then turns right and proceeds to Jay, New York, where it intersects with US Route 9N. Once you hit Route 9N (at the "four corners" in Jay), proceed through the intersection and down the hill. A sign to the "covered bridge" points the way at the intersection. The bridge is about 0.25 mile beyond the four corners. Parking is available at the bridge.

ATTRACTIONS OF ONEIDA COUNTY

WOODSMEN'S FIELD DAYS (BOONVILLE)

Lumberjack festivals and competitions aren't an uncommon event in communities across the United States. In fact, a Google search of "Lumberjack Festival" turns up almost 15 million hits. Yet very few of these rural, rustic gatherings generate as much attention as the Woodsmen's Field Days event in Boonville, New York.

Chainsaw carving competitor producing an animal figure at Woodsmen's Field Days in Boonville.

To the uninitiated, the sheer size of this festival is staggering. For the author, who was used to the small, community-based "friendly competition" type of lumberjack event, the first glimpse was beyond belief. A full grandstand and stadium-sized field filled with equipment and participants were just the start. From there, the grounds expanded into an endless sea of tents and buildings filled with industry-related materials.

"This event has taken many years to evolve and grow into what we are today," said Phyllis White, executive coordinator of New York State Woodsmen's Field Days, Inc. "We got our start way back in 1948, when Reverend Frank A. Reed first kicked things off. He was an amazing man; a pastor from Old Forge who served the lumberjacks back in the remote logging camps of the region. He wanted to give the lumberjacks an alternative to the bars and saloons of the cities, so he set up the first meet as a friendly competition, just for fun. And it's just grown beyond belief since then."

Although the festival originally moved between various locations in its early years, it eventually became shared between Tupper Lake and Boonville,

Competitor in a loader/stacker competition attempting to beat the clock in stacking a pile of log cuttings.

PHOTO BY LARRY WEILL

which alternated years as host until 1971. At that point, it moved to Boonville on a permanent basis, and the town now relishes its role as the perennial host.

"The town and surrounding area has absolutely adopted this as a permanent part of the community" said White. "To show you the level of commitment we have here, the festival has 787 volunteers who actively work on the event. And by the way, those 787 volunteers represent four generations of local families! They do everything from setup to judging to traffic control and security. There's a lot that goes into it, and the entire community is behind it."

Competitors come to the Boonville festival from every county in New York State, plus 11 other states (including at least one contestant from California). Although most of the lumberjacks are from the eastern United States, the event has attracted participants from the international scene as well, with entries from New Zealand, Australia, Germany, and even the Czech Republic.

If you decide to visit, expect to see a lot of people, as the attendance now exceeds 40,000 visitors. This number took a leap in 2014, when the event coordinators decided to add new camping areas around the vicinity.

Log cutter/splitter equipment on display in the exhibition area of the Woodsmen's Field Days.
Photo by Larry Weill

When asked how the Boonville festival differs from other lumberjack events around the country, White was quick to point out that it is unique in the scope of the business. "It's not just the fact that we're a long-standing, traditional event, which we are," she said. "But we're also a full-fledged industry trade show, with 250 companies represented. These companies provide the full range of apparatus, supplies, and support for foresting and timber harvesting, equipment, tools, and technology. It is a major draw to those people who are in the business, and a good number of deals happen right here on our grounds."

The Woodsmen's Field Days is also known for including competitions for everyone, including judged events for women and children. Events include traditional lumberjack functions such as log rolling, chain sawing, and axe throwing, as well as other contests such as a 10K road race. Food is available at many vendor locations, while other happenings (music and a fashion show!) fill out the rest of the agenda.

The festival takes place in mid-August and is very reasonably priced (a three-day pass to the entire weekend is only $27.00, with daily admissions set at $9.00 for an adult, $7.00 for children). Parking is available within walking distance, and restrooms and other conveniences are situated throughout the grounds.

The address is 222 Schuyler Street, Boonville, New York 13309. For more information, call in advance at 315-942-4593 or visit www.WoodsmensField Days.com.

H. P. SEARS OIL COMPANY, INC. MUSEUM

The "filling station," located on a busy intersection in downtown Rome, New York, looks so perfect and intact, it's a wonder more people don't try to pull in to fill their tanks. (Wood 4-by-4-inch posts prevent cars from actually pulling up to the pumps.) But the pristine appearance of the gas pumps and the superb preservation of the facility do enhance the "open-for-business" façade of the North George Street station.

The man behind the scenes of this wonderful operation is Pat Corbett, a retired newspaper reporter and dedicated volunteer. He also served a full career in the US Army and has been active in the community throughout his lifetime. "I wrote for the Utica *Observer Dispatch*, and one of the last stories I wrote was about the Sears Service Station. That's what first got me interested in this place, and I've been here ever since."

The founder of the business, Howard P. Sears Sr., was an entrepreneurial genius who started his first business around 1910 at the age of 14. He discovered a way to obtain damaged bicycles in the city of Utica and then transport them

174

Outside the Sears Oil Company Museum in Rome.
PHOTO BY LARRY WEILL

back to his house for free. There, he made the necessary repairs and sold them at a large profit. Thus, the H. P. Sears Cycle Co. was born.

Sears's next step was to graduate to procuring parts for the rapidly developing automobile market. "When a customer purchased a new car back then, all they really got was the frame," explained Corbett. "Everything else had to be purchased separately and then installed later." So Sears transitioned from bicycles to auto parts, which was a much more lucrative business.

In 1920, Howard acquired a gasoline delivery truck, which marked his entry into the fuel business. Shortly thereafter he opened a series of filling stations, beginning with one on Oriskany Blvd. in Utica and expanding out from there. The museum building on North George Street in Rome was opened in 1929. The chain eventually expanded until there were 15 to 16 locations spread between Camillus and Little Falls. Sears's two sons, Howard P. Sears Jr. and Thomas Sears, also became involved in running the business. The company eventually acquired oil barges to transport fuels to depots across the Erie Canal. It was a large and profitable business, and Howard Sr. kept his hand in all aspects of its operations until his death in 1984.

In later years, the service stations became a less important part of the overall business, and the station on North George Street was closed in 1974. It was

Photo of Sears's first pumping station, on North George Street in Rome.

vacant until 2005, when Howard Jr. acted on his long-held vision to turn it into a service station museum. The idea took hold, funded by the Sears family, and it has remained open as a museum providing a portal into the gasoline business of the 1920s.

"It's a wonderful way to get an up-close view into a different era," said Corbett. "Everything you see here is 100% original. Even the clock on the wall and the oil cans on the display case came from this station. Nothing has been recreated, although the pumps themselves were restored to their original condition."

Unfortunately, the museum does have one problem, and that is a lack of volunteers to provide coverage for visitation. "We used to have a group of about 25 volunteers who would keep this place open during the week. We had regular hours, and you could drop in unannounced whenever you wanted. Today, I'm the only one left, so I work mostly by appointment. But if you want to see the place, just call my cell phone and I'll make sure you can get in."

The museum is located at 201 North George Street, Rome, New York. There is no charge for admission, although donations are always appreciated. You can reach Pat Corbett to set up a visit at 315-335-5633. You can also email him at scoopercorbett@yahoo.com. Like most enthusiasts, he is a friendly, outgoing person who is ready to share his knowledge (which is incredibly in-depth) with anyone who is interested in learning. So feel free to stop in to the 1920s!

ATTRACTIONS OF WASHINGTON COUNTY

SASQUATCH-CALLING FESTIVAL IN WHITEHALL

For more than 200 years, the legendary Bigfoot creature has gained fame across North America as a large, hairy creature who appears out of nowhere, makes a scene in front of one or two spectators, then vanishes into the wilds from where it came. Many people claim to have seen or heard one, although no definitive proof (of a deceased one or otherwise) has ever been presented. Even the photographs that are shared frequently online are out of focus or obscured, with no really credible image available to dispel the notion that this creature is anything more than imaginary.

Bigfoot lives! Here he is, live, at the Sasquatch-Calling Festival in Whitehall. Photo by Larry Weill

However, none of this stops the good folks who attend the annual Sasquatch-Calling Festival in Whitehall, New York. This festival, which was started by Dave Molenar in 2015, serves as an attraction to people all over the area, including many from outside New York State, to come together for a good time and good food, and to visit with their favorite hairy beast.

The current director, Barbara Spoor, has noted that the festival has grown significantly since its inception and now draws over 2,000 people each year. "This has been a one-day event in each of our initial years," said Spoor. "However, there is a strong possibility that we will extend it to fill the two-day weekend next year. People really seem to enjoy it, and we have the support to make it run a full two days."

Participant in the Sasquatch-calling contest.
PHOTO BY LARRY WEILL

The festival takes place in the park alongside the Champlain Canal in downtown Whitehall and uses the park pavilion building as well as the stone amphitheater. The park is filled with exhibitors and vendors selling everything from food and drink to books, jewelry, and other Bigfoot-related souvenirs.

Of special interest are the many visitors who claim to have had a run-in with a real, live Bigfoot. The town of Whitehall appears to be a hotbed of such Sasquatch activity, and the community is loaded with signs and other references to the local Bigfoot population.

The main event of the festival is, of course, the Sasquatch-calling competition, which usually features over 100 people doing their best and scariest high-volume screams. The contest is divided into two divisions, children and adults, with prizes being awarded to each. The judging is done by a blind panel, facing the other direction, who cannot see the identity of each caller. Anyone is welcome to join the competition, so if you decide to attend this festival, keep your best screaming (or screeching or hollering) voice available and take your best shot!

The festival is usually held over the last weekend in September (in 2019 it was still Saturday only). Both admission and parking are free of charge.

For more information, visit https://www.lakegeorge.com/event/sasquatch -calling-festival-132002/ (or other websites). But be careful; there have been other Sasquatch festivals around the country, so make sure the one you find is the Whitehall, New York, event.

Plaster casting of a Bigfoot foot-print. The coin placed on the print is a silver dollar (for comparison).
PHOTO BY LARRY WEILL

ORIGINAL HOME OF PIE À LA MODE

The concept is so simple: Take one scoop of vanilla ice cream and place it on top of one slice of apple pie, and voila! There you have it: pie à la mode.

This popular American dessert has been a staple in restaurants for so long that many people do not realize it did not exist until 1896. Even then, it took a music professor, an upstate New York hotel, and some interesting happenings to make it a national dish.

The story goes that a local music teacher, Professor Charles Watson Townsend, dined on a regular basis at the restaurant of the Cambridge Hotel in Cambridge, New York. One evening Townsend decided to request ice cream on top of his favorite apple pie, which was a unique and novel idea at the time. A nearby diner, Mrs. Berry Hall, observed the concoction and exclaimed "pie à la mode," with the final words meaning "in the fashion." The term ended up sticking, and a new dessert was born.

The Cambridge Assisted Living Facility, once known as the Cambridge Hotel, original home of pie à la mode.
PHOTO BY LARRY WEILL

Townsend later made mention of the term pie à la mode in his travels in New York City and other locations, thus spreading the popularity of his new dessert across the country.

Years later, the kitchen staff of the Cambridge Hotel still took pride in being "the birthplace of pie à la mode." They often pointed out to restaurant customers the table where Professor Townsend sat when he ordered the now-famous dessert.

The original Cambridge Hotel building still stands in the small community of Cambridge,

Newspaper articles explaining the origins of pie à la mode, on display in the lobby of the Cambridge Assisted Living Facility.
PHOTO BY LARRY WEILL

New York. The town has a little more than 2,000 residents and has gradually declined in size over the past few decades.

The hotel, which was built and opened in 1885, went through several periods of decline and restoration over the years. It was finally closed as a hotel in 2012 and sold in 2014, then rebuilt into an assisted living facility in 2016.

The assisted living facility remains in operation today, providing a critical service to the elderly citizens of the area. It is *not* open to the public, and it is requested that people who are not there specifically to visit residents of the facility do not attempt to enter. However, if you happen to be passing by 4 West Main Street in Cambridge, it is still an interesting sight to view from your car.

SKENESBOROUGH MUSEUM

The town of Whitehall, New York, is so small and quiet that many passersby do not recognize its place in US history. They also are unaware of the locality's reputation as the "Birthplace of the American Navy." Gaining recognition of this fact is an objective of the Skenesborough Museum, which is located in Whitehall.

Remains of the USS *Ticonderoga*, captured by the British and later decommissioned in 1816. It was raised from the bottom of East Bay in 1958. The exhibit sits outside the Skenesborough Museum in Whitehall.

Photo by Larry Weill

The museum is loaded with exhibits that focus on both the area's naval history and its industrial and social backgrounds. The naval portion of this history is told via both artifacts and an interactive presentation and display. The presentation is accompanied by a waterfront representation of the early days along the southern end of Lake Champlain.

Through the presentation, visitors can gain an appreciation for the shipbuilding activity that led to the first naval engagements between the British and American forces. The characters British businessman Philip Skene and American Generals Philip Schuyler and Benedict Arnold come to life through these displays.

The museum's naval focus was given a huge boost with the visit of William Franke, who served as America's secretary of the navy from 1959 to 1961. During his

Interactive exhibit showing shipbuilding activity on Lake Champlain in 1776.
PHOTO BY LARRY WEILL

visit he donated a number of items that are still on display on the museum's first floor.

The rest of the museum, not dedicated to the origins of the US Navy, is used to display artifacts of local business, culture, and personalities of the Lake Champlain region. These include displays of transportation, firefighting equipment, carriages, medical devices, and more.

The Skenesborough Museum is only open during the summer months, beginning on June 2, 2023. "The building is built of concrete, so it gets very cold in the winter," said Jay Diresta, who serves as the volunteer staff coordinator.

The museum's director is Robert H. Mowatt III, who also serves as the president of the Whitehall Historical Society. "At-

William B. Franke, secretary of the navy and patron of the Skenesborough Museum.
PHOTO BY LARRY WEILL

Main exhibit hall of the Skenesborough Museum.
PHOTO BY LARRY WEILL

tendance has been down these past few years, starting with the pandemic," said Mowatt. "However, we do get visitors from around the country and throughout the world. The dedicated staff has worked to keep the museum open to the public during the summer months."

The address is 37 Skenesborough Dr., Whitehall, New York. Hours of operation are Wednesday through Saturday 11 a.m.–4 p.m. and Sunday from noon–4 p.m. These hours change every year. Visit the museum's website at https://skenesborough.com/skenesborough-museum/ or call 518-499-0716 to confirm hours of operation.

OLD FORT HOUSE MUSEUM

When first developing the outline for this book on unusual Adirondack attractions, I noticed the lack of mention of the region's involvement with the Underground Railroad. This museum, while not an integral part of the Underground Railroad, once served as the early residence of one of America's best-known escaped slaves.

Solomon Northup was born in Minerva, New York, in 1807 or 1808. His father (Mintus Northup) was a freed slave, and Solomon started his life as a free man as well. Mintus moved to the area around Fort Edward somewhere between 1816 and 1818. (Detailed records are not in existence, so the exact dates are not available.)

Solomon married Ann, who moved to Fort Edward in 1828. The couple rented a room on the second floor of the Fort House, which has been preserved as part of the museum. It's a small living space that is surrounded by other rooms, all of which were rented to other tenants.

The Old Fort House
Museum in Fort Edward.
PHOTO BY LARRY WEILL

Solomon and Ann only lived in the house for a couple years. Mintus passed away in 1829, and Solomon moved out of the Fort House the following year to take care of his mother.

Solomon was employed in several jobs throughout the 1820s, including farming and as a laborer on the Champlain Canal. He was also an accomplished violinist, which led to one of the defining moments of his life. In 1841, he was lured to Washington, DC, with prospects of employment as a traveling musician. However, the offer was a ruse, and he was kidnapped and taken to Louisiana, where he was sold into slavery. He remained there until a Canadian worker on the plantation helped him by contacting a local lawyer (Henry B. Northup, no relation), who contacted the governor of New York (Washington Hunt) to negotiate his freedom in 1851.

After regaining his status as a free man, Solomon Northup wrote and published his famous memoir, *Twelve Years a Slave*. He gained a degree of fame traveling around the country talking about his book and his experiences in Louisiana. However, by the 1860s he had vanished from public life and was no longer counted on the 1860 Census. His wife claimed that he was deceased by 1870, but nothing is known about the final years of his life or about his burial site.

Courtroom in the Old Fort House Museum.
PHOTO BY LARRY WEILL

183

The Old Fort House Museum (and campus) includes a great many exhibits and materials other than those connected with Solomon Northup. "This place truly is a piece of Revolutionary War Colonial history," said R. Paul McCarty, who serves as director of the Old Fort House Museum. "People who have visited this house include George Washington, British General John Burgoyne, Benedict Arnold, and Baroness Von Riedesel. The house was completed in 1772, and is the oldest frame building in Washington County."

The museum is a popular tourist destination and draws 3,000–4,000 visitors per year. It also offers educational programs to local schools and groups. There are also other buildings on the "campus," including a toll house, a one-room schoolhouse, an 1850s law office, and an 1870s county fair building.

The address is 29 Broadway, Fort Edward, New York. The museum is open during the summer from June through mid-October. For more on the museum's hours, visit oldforthousemuseum.com or call 518-747-9600.

THE ONLY LAVENDER FARM IN THE ADIRONDACKS

The ancient stone house sits alone on the side of a quiet road in the town of Whitehall, New York. A large stone above the front entrance displays a year: 1820. It's an old house that is inhabited by a couple of new residents. Matt and Linda Smith, newly transplanted from New Paltz, New York, purchased the house in 2022 without any knowledge of the beautiful crop growing right in their own backyard.

Ancient house on Deweys Bridge Road in Whitehall, home to Lavenlair Farm.
PHOTO BY LARRY WEILL

"We lived on a property in New Paltz where we raised Percheron draft horses," explained Matt. "When we bought the house and came up here for the first time, we saw all the flowers growing in the back field and didn't know what we had. It wasn't until later that we discovered we now owned a lavender farm."

The Smiths wanted to open a business on their new property, as they needed to roll over the proceeds from their previous business into a new endeavor. However, they hadn't expected to have this new "floral opportunity" presented as a ready-to-run farm.

The Smiths also discovered that there is more than one variety of lavender plant. In fact, the genus Lavandula includes about 47 different species, which are broken down into five main varieties: English lavender, French lavender, Lavandin, Portuguese lavender, and Spanish lavender. Each has slightly different requirements for treatment and care.

"We found out that the 'New Zealand Blue' holds up best in our Adirondack climate," said Matt. "But some of the varieties, especially the French lavender, died off because the plants weren't covered for the winter."

Once the Smiths get the farm up and running, they plan on opening a store on the premises and offering a variety of products and dried blooms for

Rows of lavender plants growing in the fields of Lavenlair Farm.
Photo by Larry Weill

sale to the public. They also want to open the farm to "U-pick" activities at least a couple days a week.

Another old structure on the farm is a one-room schoolhouse that also once served as a church. The Smiths plan on refurbishing this building and using it to house a working museum, complete with photographs and artifacts from the early days of the 1800s. They also want to use it to demonstrate how the various products on Lavenlair Farm are produced from the lavender plants.

Lavenlair Farm is a beautiful place that will offer your family a window into the "olden days" of this specialized form of crop farming. Matt and Linda Smith are a charming couple who will be sure to show you a wonderful time and teach you about this beautiful flower. To find their business, visit https://lavenlairfarm.com or call 518-586-4707.

ATTRACTIONS OF HERKIMER COUNTY

MURDER ON BIG MOOSE LAKE: THE GRACE BROWN TRAGEDY

Perhaps one of the most famous incidents ever to occur inside the Adirondack Park was the 1906 murder of Grace Mae Brown, a 20-year-old factory worker from the central heartland of New York. Born in the small farming community of South Otselic, New York, in 1886, she later moved to Cortland to live with her sister and work in the Gillette Skirt factory.

While employed at the factory, she fell into a relationship with the factory owner's nephew, Chester Gillette. The relationship was ill-fated from the beginning, as Gillette came from a prominent moneyed family while Brown was

Big Moose Station Restaurant, site of the train station where Grace Brown and Chester Gillette arrived prior to their fateful ride on the lake. Built in 1926; original station burned down in 1923.

Photo by Larry Weill

a simple factory worker, who would not have suited Gillette's family's ideas of an appropriate spouse.

In early 1906, Grace became pregnant with Gillette's child and began making forceful overtures to him about marriage. She began writing letters on a daily basis expressing her love for him and, later, stressing her desire for him to accept responsibility for her pregnancy. It was this activity that moved Gillette to begin planning her demise.

Gillette lured Brown to Big Moose, New York, in July 1906, where he checked them into the Glenmore Hotel using an assumed name. He then took her out onto the lake in a small canoe, supposedly as part of a prehoneymoon excursion. Sometime during that boat ride, he struck her over the head (supposedly with a tennis racket) and then threw her body overboard. He then paddled back to shore, leaving no witnesses to the crime.

Brown's body was discovered the next day, and authorities quickly discovered her identity and her developing pregnancy. They also surmised that Chester Gillette was the prime suspect and confiscated her accumulated love letters from his room. He was promptly arrested in the town of Inlet the following day.

Historic marker for the Grace Brown murder saga on Big Moose Lake.

<small>Photo by Larry Weill</small>

The murder case went to trial in November 1906 and resulted in Gillette's sentencing and eventual execution in 1908. One of the most compelling pieces of evidence was the pile of love letters, in which Grace Brown repeatedly sought to convince Chester to marry her. The final letter, written six days before her death, raised the possibility that she might soon be approaching the end of her life. Her premonition came true when Chester Gillette murdered her on July 11 on Big Moose Lake.

Grace Brown's murder has been preserved for posterity in Joseph Brownell and Patricia Wawrzaszek's *Adirondack Tragedy: The Gillette Murder Case of 1906* and Craig

Big Moose Lake as it appears today, photographed from next to the boathouse.

<small>Photo by Larry Weill</small>

Original undated photo of the Glenmore Hotel boathouse in Big Moose.
PUBLIC DOMAIN

The boathouse as it appears today.
PHOTO BY LARRY WEILL

Brando's *Murder in the Adirondacks: An American Tragedy Revisited*. Both were published in 1986.

The original Glenmore Hotel burned down in 1950, leaving the boathouse as the only surviving structure that bore witness to the crime.

To find Big Moose Lake, follow NY Route 28 north past Old Forge to the town of Eagle Bay. In Eagle Bay, turn left onto Big Moose Road and travel an additional 6 miles, then turn right onto Glenmore Road. The historic marker is lakeside at the end of this road.

MOSS LAKE REBELLION OF 1974

Driving northeast from Eagle Bay on Big Moose Road, most tourists don't stop to give the trailhead marker a second look. It simply reads "Moss Lake Trailhead Parking" and appears no different from any other parking lot and recreational area. Yet this spot was the scene of a confrontation in 1974 that had its roots in the early years of our country.

The history of the confiscatory land grabs from the indigenous Native American tribes in New York State is lengthy and complex, dating back to the original treaties approved by Governor George Clinton in the 1780s. Treaty after treaty was proposed and signed by the state and federal governments, all of

Moss Lake Trailhead sign outside Eagle Bay.
PHOTO BY LARRY WEILL

189

which accumulated (or "leased") massive tracts of lands with very little provided in remuneration. These lands were then distributed or sold to individual white settlers, who have become firmly entrenched over the past more than 200 years, long beyond their reasonable expectations of eminent domain.

The purpose of this text is not to provide an authoritative accounting of these transactions, but rather to describe the circumstances behind the eventual boiling over of tensions and confrontation. The Iroquois Nation has disputed many of the original treaties as being invalid for numerous reasons and has pressed its legal case for the return of several tracts of land across New York State, although little has been done to address the complaints.

In 1974, a group of Mohawk Indians took over an area including a girls' camp, which encompassed approximately 612 acres along the shores of Moss Lake (or Ganienkeh), outside of Eagle Bay, New York. The group maintained that the land was rightfully theirs by treaty, and they intended to remain. Although no official action was taken to remove the band from the land, frictions existed between the local population and the Mohawks encamped on the Moss Lake property. After claiming that they had been fired upon from cars passing by, the Mohawks fired back, which resulted in two injuries, including to a nine-year-old girl who was shot in the back.

A partial resolution was worked out in the Moss Lake Agreement of 1977, in which the Mohawks were provided with permanent possession to some lands situated in eastern Clinton County, about 15 miles west of Lake Champlain. They completed their relocation in 1978, and the state removed the last of its buildings in 1979.

Moss Lake, photographed from near the east end of the lake.

Photo by Larry Weill

Today, Moss Lake is a recreational hiking and boating area that is circled by a 3-mile loop trail. The lake also offers numerous camping sites, three of which are boat accessible. To reach Moss Lake, follow Big Moose Road approximately 3 miles north from the junction with NY Route 28 in Eagle Bay. The parking lot is on the left side of the road and is well marked.

LLAMAS LIVE HERE!

One thing really stands out from the moment you set foot on the Moose River Farm in Old Forge, New York—Anne Phinney *really* loves animals. Anne came from a background in education, serving as a teacher in the area around Old Forge, New York. Residents in the town still remember her fondly as their teacher when they were growing up in the small Adirondack community.

Sign on the road welcoming visitors to Moose River Farm, Old Forge.
PHOTO BY LARRY WEILL

Anne retired from her job in the local school system in 2018. She had already launched her "retired career" working with creatures both big and small on the fledgling farm that was built by her husband Rod. From 2000 to 2004, Rod steadfastly worked to raise the structures that would later blossom into the business that exists today. It was a labor of love that they both enjoy to this day.

Anne originally had in mind to develop a business for the main purpose of providing a venue for children to interact with animals. At first she worked primarily with horses, which she trained in the large training arena at the back of the farm. She also adopted a trio of goats, which she hand raised and bottle fed from newborns to adulthood. (She still refers to these three goats as "her daughters," and they have free rein

Anne Phinney with three of her "girl" llamas.
PHOTO PROVIDED COURTESY OF ANNE PHINNEY

over the barn and farm.) Donkeys, and of course llamas, also grace the farm acres, along with a multitude of smaller animals. Regardless of the species, Anne loves them all.

In 2017, Anne adopted her first three llamas, and she immediately fell in love with these sociable and affectionate creatures. Each has been given a name, and Anne is intimately familiar with their characteristics and personalities. "They really are such loving animals," she remarked as one of them leaned over to nuzzle the side of her neck. There were 10 llamas in residence on the farm when I visited.

The farm provides a host of activities for visitors, whether they are familiar with llamas or not. The featured activity at Moose River Farm is the llama trek, which is designed for enthusiasts of all ages. The standard length llama trek is a 1-mile walk that takes about 45 minutes and is combined with a 45-minute farm tour. For children younger than age eight, Anne recommends a shorter trek to accommodate their shorter attention span. Llama treks can be scheduled regardless of the season, so winter dates can be accommodated as well as summer. (The llamas enjoy being outside in all seasons!) All these hikes are conducted on trails that crisscross the 77 acres of land belonging to the farm. Prices for all the treks and activities are extremely reasonable and can be discussed when you make your reservation.

Llamas inside the training arena.
Photo by Larry Weill

Visits to the llama farm (and the llama treks) book up early, so you'll need to call a couple weeks early to ensure a reservation. In addition to the llama treks, the farm also does farm tours, a Kids' Farm Day, and custom birthday parties. Anne, who is also a published author, also conducts "author visits" on which you can discuss her works and purchase signed copies of her two books.

The address is 168 Woodcraft Road, Old Forge, New York. For more information, visit www.mooseriverfarm.com. You can also email Anne at mooseriverfarm@gmail.com or call 315-860-0222.

MINING FOR DIAMONDS IN HERKIMER

There is somehow something very alluring about mining for precious items, such as gold, silver, and gemstones. Unfortunately, the state of New York does not permit people to keep any gold or silver they may find, even on their own property. This statute dates back to "The King's Law," which is part of the State Constitution of 1775. (That's right, before we were even a country!)

Fortunately, there are other items of value that can be mined in the state of New York, and one of them is found at the Herkimer Diamond Mine facility, located at 4626 NY-28, Herkimer, New York. The phone number is

Entrance to Herkimer Diamond Miner's Village in Herkimer.
Photo by Larry Weill

Road leading to the exposed rock surfaces and loose stones containing the Herkimer diamonds.
Photo by Larry Weill

315-891-3099. The "Herkimer Diamond" is a "double-terminated quartz crystal" that resembles a real diamond, right down to the sparkle. Owned by the Scialdo family for the past 50 years, the facility attracts would-be treasure hunters and gem enthusiasts from a wide swath of the country.

The actual mine, where the public is permitted to search, is at the end of a short dirt road leading to exposed rock walls and piles of broken stones. Some of the loose rocks have an unusual feature: They contain porous-looking holes, which are called "vugs" (although some call them "bugs"). It is inside these openings that people sometimes find the beautiful crystals.

People interested in hunting for Herkimer diamonds may do so using a variety of methods. The most popular of these is to use one of the rock hammers available in the entrance building. These are used to pound on promising-looking rocks until they break open, exposing the crystals inside. Others like to "surface hunt," especially after periods of heavy rain that wash away the layer of dust that hides the gems. Still others prefer the "sluice" method, which involves purchas-

Herkimer diamonds for sale in the facility's gift shop. (U.S. quarter shown for perspective.)
Photo by Larry Weill

194

ing bags of premined material which is then washed to remove the dirt from the gemstones. This is probably the easiest method, although it does involve the additional cost of the bagged material.

"This is our second time up here," said Don Meyer, a resident of Pensacola, FL, who has enjoyed searching for gemstones around the world with his wife, Rita. "We had a great time during our last visit, which was right after a heavy rain storm. There were crystals exposed all over the top layer of rocks, so we didn't have to do nearly as much work with the hammer. We've shopped for stones at mineral shows in France, Germany, and throughout the United States. We've also tried our hand at mining for gems at the Crater of Diamonds Park in Arkansas and at the Ron Coleman Quartz Mine, which is also in Arkansas. But Herkimer has given us some of the best results anywhere. We love coming here."

The Herkimer Diamond Mine is actually a complete complex of buildings, campgrounds, stores, an educational center, and more. The gift shop alone is worth an extended visit and contains a huge variety of stones and completed jewelry pieces. However, the staff is quick to point out that not all the stones offered for sale in the shop are from the Herkimer Diamond Mine. They also work with suppliers from a great many locations to offer the greatest variety.

If you decide to visit the Herkimer Diamond Mine, there are a number of things you should know while planning your visit. The first is that the facility takes safety very seriously and requires personal safety attire including closed-toe shoes, safety glasses, and more. Gloves are also recommended, especially if using a hammer and chisel. Consult the website for a complete list of requirements.

For those who can't get enough prospecting in a single day, the facility also offers a wide variety of camping options, which range from tent sites and RV sites to different levels of private cabins. For more on these options, visit the website at https://herkimerdiamond.com.

ATTRACTIONS OF SARATOGA COUNTY

PRESIDENT ULYSSES S. GRANT'S LAST RESIDENCE

Most people have never heard of the town of Wilton, New York, much less the geographic prominence of Mt. McGregor. Yet almost every schoolchild knows about General Ulysses S. Grant and his role in the American Civil War.

The connection between the man and the place is forever linked due to the presence of a small yellow cottage that doesn't receive the recognition it is due. The Ulysses S. Grant Cottage, located at 1000 Mt. McGregor Road, Gansevoort,

Cabin in Wilton, home to President Ulysses S. Grant during the final months of his life, taken in July 1885.

Historic marker for the Ulysses S. Grant Cottage.
PHOTO BY LARRY WEILL

Photograph of Grant's image that hangs inside the Grant Cottage.
PHOTO BY LARRY WEILL

New York, is where the famous Civil War general lived out his final days in his race to finish his memoirs before his death from cancer in the summer of 1885.

The cabin and its surrounding grounds are sufficiently scenic to create their own memories. The land, which originally served as a picnic grounds for the local church organization, later held numerous other buildings, including a large hotel (the Balmoral) that featured some of the first electrical power in the area. The land changed hands several times, both before and after Grant's tenure at the cottage. The cottage itself was relocated in 1883 to make room for the larger hotel, which later burned in 1897.

Former president Grant's time at the cabin was a painful race against death. Battling cancer of the throat, he was attended to by a cadre of physicians who could do little to improve his condition. He often sat on the porch outside the cottage as he recorded his memoirs of his life as Lincoln's commanding general during the Civil War. During this time, Grant had the assistance of one of America's most beloved writers and storytellers, Mark Twain. The dying former president had been swindled out of his family's financial assets by several unscrupulous parties, and he faced the prospect of seeing his family having to live in relative poverty unless he could complete his memoirs, which would provide a lifetime of royalty payments. Grant was a man of integrity and principle, and he knew that was a race he simply could not lose.

Grant moved into the cottage on June 16, 1885, and the final six weeks of his life were consumed by his writing. Aided by Mark Twain, who provided Grant with a $25,000 payment in exchange for the completed memoirs, Grant persisted despite experiencing great pain. Unable to eat much due to his worsening condition, he continued until the writing was complete, which was a scant three days before his death on July 23, 1885.

Room in which President Grant died in July 1885. The furniture and contents of the cottage have remained intact, preserved for posterity.

PHOTO BY LARRY WEILL

Visitors today can tour the cabin, which is attended by a full-time caretaker. This attendant is well versed in all aspects of the cabin and its famous resident of almost 140 years ago. The site is located on a very passable road and is situated about 9 miles outside of Saratoga Springs, New York. Adult tickets cost $12.00, with discounts available for students and seniors. Children and military personnel (including veterans) are not charged a fee.

The cottage is closed through the winter months but reopens in May and remains open into October. Tours last approximately 30 minutes and can be booked online. (No one can enter the cottage without purchasing a tour pass.) Visit https://grantcottage.org/hours to book tickets. You can also call 518-584-4353 for more information.

THE ABNER DOUBLEDAY HOUSE

Most Americans aren't thoroughly familiar with many of our country's historical figures. However, one name that most of us recognize is Abner Doubleday, the assumed founder of American baseball.

Doubleday was born in the town of Ballston Spa, New York, in 1819. The house where he was born and spent his early years still stands at the corner of Washington and Fenwick Streets (although there is some historical debate as to whether he actually resided in this building). The house was built in 1804 and is the last remaining structure of the Sans Souci hotel complex erected on the site. The hotel was in operation until 1849 and was finally torn down in 1887.

Abner Doubleday House (now also known as The Real McCoy), in Ballston Spa.
Photo by Larry Weill

Abner Doubleday went on to have an illustrious and diverse career following his childhood years in Ballston Spa. He rose to the rank of major general in the US Army, served with distinction at the Battle of Gettysburg, and was credited with firing the first shot in the defense of Fort Sumter. Later, in 1905, the Mills Commission credited Doubleday with being the originator of baseball, which has also been disputed by contemporary scholars of the sport. One additional footnote to add to his lifelong accomplishments is his founding of the Cable Car Company of San Francisco, California.

Major General Abner Doubleday in army uniform.

Public domain

Following the Doubledays' residence in the house on Washington Street, the building went through a number of owners and tenants as the surrounding neighborhood changed. A gentleman known as "Ice Cream Pete" Parrelle bought the structure in 1922 and completed a thorough remodeling job, which included converting it from a two-family home to a one-family dwelling. Parrelle moved out of the building in 1946, and it eventually became an empty, derelict structure.

Today's owner, local attorney and judge John Cromiy, purchased the house in the 1980s and immediately addressed some of the most critical structural problems. "The rear wall was falling out from the foundation," said Cromiy, who also serves as the town historian. "Additionally, the foundation itself was poorly

Serving room of The Real McCoy, located inside the Doubleday House.
PHOTO BY LARRY WEILL

constructed, which led to many other defects in alignment throughout the building. It required a lot of work and materials to shore up the walls and ceilings, not to mention the six fireplaces we removed during the remodeling."

Cromiy found an industrious tenant in Mike Schaffer, who converted the first floor of the 120-year-old building into a charming brew pub called The Real McCoy. (The official name is The Real McCoy Beer Co.) The small bar is configured for beer tastings and offers an array of small-batch brews made from hops and barley sourced from Upstate New York. Its offerings on tap include beers such as Empire Red Ale, Real McCoy OctoberFest, Liberty Cream Ale, and Doubleday IPA.

The address is 28 Washington Street, Ballston Spa, New York. The bar is currently only open on weekends, although Schaffer has plans to extend the hours. For more about the pub and its hours, visit the website at www.thereal mccoybeerco.com or call 518-817-7423.

Historic sign in front of the Abner Doubleday House in Ballston Spa.
PHOTO BY LARRY WEILL

BENEDICT ARNOLD: AMERICAN HERO OR TRAITOR?

Of all the figures who fought in our War of Independence, none is more polarizing than Benedict Arnold. Best remembered for being a traitor for the British, his name is synonymous with anyone who defects to the enemy side. Yet prior to his defection, Arnold served admirably in several locations and battles across our fledgling country. He also incurred the wrath of many of his contemporaries for pursuing his own personal glory, which led to disagreements and feuds with his fellow officers.

"The Boot" Monument at stop 7 of the Saratoga National Historical Park tour in Stillwater.
PHOTO BY LARRY WEILL

Born in Connecticut in 1841, Arnold displayed a talent for military strategy and leadership at an early age and played a pivotal role (along with others) in the capture of Fort Ticonderoga. His leadership in the Battle of Valcour Island on Lake Champlain in 1776 helped delay the British advance southward toward New York. He was recognized for these heroic efforts and promoted to the rank of major general, becoming one of George Washington's more trusted leaders.

During the Battle of Saratoga in 1777, Arnold was shot through his left leg, which had already been injured in an earlier skirmish. The wound put him out of service, so Washington installed him as the military commander of the city of Philadelphia. While serving in this post, he was accused of profiting from "questionable financial dealings" and also conspiring to provide military information to the British.

After being admonished by Washington for his dishonorable behavior, Arnold left Philadelphia and gained command at West Point, where he made plans to weaken the fort and turn the entire installation over to the British. Unfortu-

General Benedict Arnold.
PUBLIC DOMAIN

nately for him, his main contact with the British (John Andre) was captured and hanged, and Arnold narrowly escaped to England. There he joined the British Army for the remainder of the war. He lived in England until his death in 1801.

The Saratoga National Historical Park has a superb 9-mile road that leads visitors to all the important locations of the various skirmishes in the two Battles of Saratoga. Each of the nine numbered stops has informational signboards and displays that describe the actions that took place at that particular spot on the battlefield.

The Boot memorial, commemorating General Benedict Arnold's role at Saratoga, can be found at stop 7 on the park tour. Like most memorials to America's most famous traitor, his name does not appear on the monument. (Even where his name had appeared on plaques and other memorials, it has been scratched out or otherwise removed, as seen on the plaque which had borne his name on the wall at West Point.)

The Saratoga National Historical Park is a fascinating destination for families and anyone interested in American history. While The Boot Monument is a high point of the park, the entire battlefield is of interest because it marks a real turning point in the American Revolution.

The park is located at 648 Route 32 in Stillwater, New York. It is open year-round, and the entrance road is open from 9:00 a.m. until 5:00 p.m. daily, although the Tour Road is closed to vehicles from December through March. Open times may vary with closures for repairs and construction, so visit the website at www.nps.gov/sara/planyourvisit before you drive to the park.

View from the top of the hill outside the visitors' center at Saratoga National Historical Park. The battlefield is visible below.
Photo by Larry Weill

ATTRACTIONS OF ST. LAWRENCE COUNTY

THE GHOST THAT CAME TO BREAKFAST

The brick building that sits on Main Street in the town of Massena, New York, doesn't look much different than many other upstate restaurants. A sign on the side of the establishment simply reads "Spanky's" and lists its hours of operation, while proudly boasting of its "home cooking." But the outward appearance says little of the interesting activity that takes place inside the walls of the business.

The author's visit to this restaurant took place in August 2020, and everything was perfectly normal at that time. Breakfast consisted of a stack of pancakes with a side order of sausage, all of which was superb. The pancakes were large and delicious and were delivered to the table by a friendly and beaming waitress. (Food always tastes better with a smile.)

Spanky's Diner in Massena, known for its superb food as well is its ghostly residents.

Front dining room in Spanky's Diner. The diner does a brisk business at breakfast time.
PHOTO BY LARRY WEILL

However, some of the visitors to Spanky's are more interested in the reports of the paranormal activity that emanates from the basement. That is where the supernatural spirits (aka ghosts) are reported to hang out, a presence that has been reported for many years and by numerous sources.

The owner of the restaurant, Valerie LaValley, is the daughter of the restaurant's namesake, Spanky. The restaurant has been in the family close to 40 years, although the stories of hauntings predate the family's involvement. It turns out that the site of the diner was originally the grounds of a hospital in World War II, so some of the spirits may inhabit the location today. The owner was gracious enough to permit me to descend into the basement of the building, which is where much of the ghostly activity has been reported. It is in those darkened rooms that most of the voices, bumps, and knocks have been heard. Footsteps have been heard moving through areas where no one had been, and several doors have been known to open and close without human intervention.

Room in the basement of Spanky's Diner where supernatural voices and movement have been detected.
PHOTO BY LARRY WEILL

Much of the space inside those rooms has been set aside for storage, and several of the employees have encountered unusual sensations while moving between the spaces. Objects left in the cellar have been known to move between rooms, further complicating the mystery. Reports of multiple voices, from those of young children to an older and more sinister man, have been detected, leading some to believe that there are several spirits in residence at the restaurant.

Most of the patrons of the restaurant, as well as the staff, seem to take the hauntings in stride. While speaking to the customers, they seemed to be divided in their opinions about the presence of unearthly spirits in the building: Some believed while others did not. However, several of the waitstaff admitted to having experienced unexplainable sounds and sensations in different parts of the restaurant, from voices to footsteps and more. Regardless, most of the customers are locals, and come in for the excellent food rather than the chances of encountering an unnatural apparition.

A paranormal investigative team from the area conducted an overnight visit to Spanky's in March 2022 and reported an abundance of paranormal activity. The team of investigators positioned themselves throughout the building from closing time until morning, setting up several sensors to monitor different forms of sound and energy.

The results from the team's investigation were impressive. Quite a few voices were detected, along with bumps, footsteps, and other sounds. The activity fluctuated throughout the night, at some points reaching truly frenetic levels of activity.

Spanky's is located at 3 N. Main Street in Massena, New York. They are open from 6 a.m.–8 p.m. seven days a week. If you decide to visit, you can be certain that you'll be treated to a great home-cooked meal and friendly service. And remember, you don't have to tip the ghosts.

MASSENA'S (HAUNTED) PINE GROVE CEMETERY

It's easy to believe that a cemetery can be haunted, right? After all, it's a place where the deceased are brought for burial, so it's only natural to assume that some of those spirits may decide to hang around for a while. (This is said tongue in cheek.)

One such graveyard with a reputation for displays of the supernatural is the Pine Grove Cemetery located at 3 Prospect Park, Massena, New York. This burial site is tucked between the Raquette River, Cook Road, and Hough Road, and has a wide-open feel due to the absence of many large trees over most of the gravesites. The main gate is a wrought-iron structure with "Pine Grove Cemetery" forged in an archway over the entrance road.

Gateway to the Pine Grove Cemetery in Massena.
Photo by Larry Weill

The story that goes with this graveyard dates back to the construction of the massive dam on the St. Lawrence River, which crosses from Barnhart Island (from Massena) over to the shoreline of Canada about 50 miles southwest of Montreal. The construction of the dam necessitated the excavation and relocation of graves from at least 19 other cemeteries, which were brought to the Pine Grove Cemetery in Massena and reburied in the local plot. Visitors have reported seeing ghostly apparitions of small children playing with one another and spirits conversing and strolling through the site.

Other stories include mysterious claw marks appearing on the inside surfaces of decaying caskets, although the author was unable to find any credible references that discussed this phenomenon. Regardless, this graveyard is a beautiful and scenic location to take an afternoon stroll, with or without the presence of paranormal companions.

ATTRACTIONS OF CLINTON COUNTY

HISTORIC ISLANDS IN LAKE CHAMPLAIN: VALCOUR ISLAND

The town of Peru is a small community located about halfway up the west side of Lake Champlain. It sits about 5 miles south of Plattsburgh and is wholly contained inside Clinton County. It's a small community whose population declined somewhat between the last two census counts and now sits a bit below 6,800 residents.

View over the Peru dock across the strait to Valcour Island.
Photo by Larry Weill

The main draw of this quiet lakeside community is the history, which links the location to a key chapter of the Revolutionary War. Directly across a narrow straight of Lake Champlain from the Peru boat launch sits the historic Valcour Island. It is a small land mass, only 2 miles in length and about a mile wide. But its small dimensions are dwarfed by its huge role in the history of our nation.

Valcour Island, which is officially part of Plattsburgh, New York, is recognizable by the large red lighthouse that sits on a prominence overlooking the middle of the island. There are no roads on this island. There is nothing but this lighthouse. The Bluff Point Lighthouse was constructed in 1874 and is clearly viewed from the Peru Dock Boat Launch. Most people who visit the island enjoy hiking the trail leading up to the lighthouse building, which is well maintained by the Clinton County Historical Association.

The island has a lot more to see and visit than just the lighthouse. The land and surrounding waters gained fame through Benedict Arnold's famous engagement against a British fleet of ships led by General Guy Carleton. On October 11, 1776, after two days of sailing south on Lake Champlain, Carleton's fleet located and engaged the American gunboats, which had stationed themselves in a line off the tip of the island. The British ships were much larger and more

Bluff Point Lighthouse, on the west side of Valcour Island.
PHOTO BY LARRY WEILL

heavily armed and quickly overpowered the newly constructed American vessels. However, Arnold was able to escape under cover of night and a heavy fog, eventually leading the surviving units of his force to the relative safety of Fort Ticonderoga. Most of his ships were burned to prevent capture by the British, but Arnold was credited with stalling the British force, which returned to Canada until the following year.

Valcour Island is today owned by the state of New York. It can be accessed by a short boat ride of about 10 minutes from the Peru dock. The island contains about 7 miles of trails, including some that circumnavigate the island and others that cut across the middle.

The author enjoyed the services of a local boat captain, Mickey Maynard, who charters his boat for numerous types of excursions, including fishing and tourism. His business (Lake Champlain Angler Fishing Charters) was reasonably priced and extremely accommodating. He agreed to provide transportation not only to Valcour Island, but also to Crab Island, as part of this research project. His experience on the local waters, as well as his knowledge of the locations of the historic sites, was invaluable to this part of this book. He can be reached at 518-578-9273 or online at http://www.lakechamplainangler.com.

HISTORIC ISLANDS IN LAKE CHAMPLAIN: CRAB ISLAND

A little over a mile north up the coast from Valcour Island sits yet another historic land mass, known as Crab Island. It is distinctly smaller than Valcour Island (less than 1/20 the size) and is almost unnoticeable on maps of Lake Champlain. However, it too played an interesting role in the early history of our country.

Crab Island is an important landmark in the War of 1812, which was fought primarily over maritime rights, as well as Britain's impressment of American sailors. The war was fought between 1812 and 1814, although the last major encounter, the Battle of New Orleans, was fought in January 1815. By that time, the Treaty of Ghent (which ended the war) had been signed by both sides, though not yet ratified.

Marble obelisk on Crab Island commemorating the lives lost during the Battle of Lake Champlain.
Photo by Larry Weill

The Battle of Lake Champlain (which was part of the larger Battle of Plattsburgh) was fought on September 11, 1814. It included a British Army group, under Lieutenant General Sir George Prévost, and a naval squadron that was led by Captain George Downie. The Americans faced off against the British ships with their own squadron of warships under the command of Lieutenant Thomas Macdonough. This force included several newer vessels: the USS *Saratoga* (a 26-gun corvette), the USS *Ticonderoga* (a schooner with 14 guns), and the USS *Preble* (with 7 guns), among other smaller gunboats. The British had built a new 36-gun frigate, the HMS *Confiance*, to counter these new threats.

On the morning of September 11, 1814, Macdonough had positioned his American ship inside the Bay of Plattsburgh. It was anchored in a position to bring all of its firepower to bear upon the British ships once they arrived. Downie's squadron arrived around 10:00 a.m. but had to contend with unfavorable winds and was unable to maneuver into position. The American ships began pounding the British vessels with multiple broadsides of cannon fire, severely damaging the *Confiance*. In separate actions, the HMS *Chubb* and the HMS *Finch* were also damaged or drifted aground, thus forcing the British officers to surrender to the American naval commanders onboard USS *Saratoga*. The nautical Battle of Lake Champlain was over.

Throughout the Battle of Plattsburgh, the dead and wounded from both sides were brought to a hospital that had been hastily established on Crab Island. Some of the lesser wounded were used to man a small cannon emplacement on the island to bombard the British ships. At one time, the hospital held as many as 700 wounded soldiers and sailors, although the majority of these troops were evacuated to larger hospital facilities in Vermont.

Crab Island was used to bury about 150 men who perished during the battle. This included soldiers and sailors from both sides, and Crab Island is unique in that it is one of the few places in the world where American and British troops are buried side by side in the same mass graves. A number of memorial plaques, along with a 100-foot-tall marble obelisk, have been placed on the island to serve as reminders of those who perished during that battle.

As with Valcour Island, anyone is able to visit Crab Island as long as they can arrange boat transportation between the two islands. Once again, the author used the services of boat captain Mickey Maynard, whose boat made the run between the islands within a matter of a few minutes. Once there, the trail leading to the memorials is fairly level and easy to follow.

If you decide to visit, there are a few words of caution to heed. The first is that there is no permanent dock or pier on Crab Island, so you will probably have to climb off the boat into about a foot of water and walk over the rocky bottom of the lake, which can be slippery. Wear shoes that can withstand being submerged

CRAB ISLAND IS THE PRESUMED BURIAL SITE FOR THESE AMERICAN SEAMEN AND MARINES KILLED ON BOARD THE U.S. SQUADRON ON LAKE CHAMPLAIN, IN THE ENGAGEMENT WITH THE BRITISH FLEET, ON THE 11TH OF SEPTEMBER 1814.

Thomas Anwright	Ebeneźer Johnson	John Sellack
John Atkinson	Henry Johnson	John Sharp
David Bennett	Peter Johnson	John Smart
William Brickell	Jacob Laraway	Arthur W. Smith
Benjamin Burrill	Thomas Lewis	Samuel Smith
Thomas Butler	Jacob Lindman	Thomas Stephens
James Carlisle	Thomas Malony	Robert Stratton
John Coleman	Randall McDonald	Deodrick Think
Joseph Couch	Edward Moore	Peter Vandermere
Abraham Davis	Perkins Moore	John Wallace
James Day	Andrew Nelson	John White
John Fisher	James Norberry	Jerome Williams
Thomas Gill	Andrew Parmlee	Nace Wilson
James M. Hale	Peter Post	James Winship
Peter Hanson	John Ribero	John Wood
Joseph Heaton	Joseph Rowe	William Wyer

Plaque listing the names of the American sailors killed during the Battle of Lake Champlain.
PHOTO BY LARRY WEILL

and bring along a walking stick for balance, if needed. The other issue is the poison ivy, which grows *everywhere* on the island. The trails are well tended, so it is easy to avoid contact with the poison ivy, but you should know how to recognize the leaves to avoid walking through any of it off the trail.

NORTH STAR UNDERGROUND RAILROAD MUSEUM

This museum is unusual in many ways, including its location, its background, and its focus. First, the historical museum sits almost on top of the Ausable Chasm attraction that is visited by tens of thousands of tourists each year. It is right on the border between Clinton and Essex Counties. Looking at the building from the middle of the bridge on US Route 9, it looks as though it is ready to topple into the gorge at any moment.

The focus of the museum is the routes and passageways followed by escaped slaves on their way through the Champlain region en route to Quebec and Ontario, Canada. While there are numerous individual stopping places on the

Front view of the North Star Underground Railroad Museum in Ausable Chasm.
PHOTO BY LARRY WEILL

underground railroad that can be located throughout the area, this museum ties everything together with informative maps, artifacts, and displays throughout the building.

As museums go, this one is relatively new. It was the brainchild of Don and Vivian Papson and was started in 2010. "The building itself dates back to the 1880s," said Larry Hobson, one of the museum's volunteer guides. "But it is

Shackles found in the Chinese detention center in Port Henry. This was the site of a Chinese jail built on the "Chinese Underground Railroad," which is part of this exhibit.
PHOTO BY LARRY WEILL

important to note that this building had nothing to do with the Underground Railroad. It was simply an empty building that had fallen into disrepair and was donated by the Town of Chesterfield."

"The house was built by Herbert Estes, who was the Superintendent of the Ausable Chasm Horse Nails Work Factory," said Jackie Madison. Madison serves as the president of the North Country Underground Railroad Historical Association.

Several of the exhibits in the museum point out the divisive influence that slavery had on the local churches. Wendell Lansing, a member of the local Baptist Church, was also the editor of the newspaper. He tried to have supporters of slavery banned from the local church. He fought in the Civil War and was captured by the Confederates. During his captivity, he maintained a diary that was read to Congress after he was freed.

Later on, the town of Chesterfield gained ownership of the house, which it donated to start a heritage center. Don Papson later convinced the town to dedicate part of the building as a museum to commemorate the Underground Railroad. This plan was adopted, and the building opened as a joint operation in 2011. In 2019, the town of Chesterfield donated the building to the museum, and the North Star Underground Railroad Museum was established as an independent entity. The museum has gained the complete support of the town and functions dually as a museum and a heritage center. It receives about 6,000 visitors a year.

The museum is located at 131 Mace Chasm Road, Ausable Chasm, New York. For more information, visit https://northcountryundergroundrailroad.com or call 518-834-5180.

ACKNOWLEDGMENTS

More than any book I've undertaken, this project could not have been possible without the assistance of countless wonderful people. I have done my best to keep track of all those who aided my research as I traveled the length and breadth of the Adirondack Park, but there may be a few whose names never made it to these pages, and for this I offer my sincerest apologies in advance.

Many of the individuals who freely volunteered their time and contributory research hours were designated historians for their respective towns and counties. These scholars were invaluable in multiple ways, not only answering questions on specific ruins and remains but also suggesting topics for inclusion that I never would have foreseen. The county historians were especially valuable in directing me to the historic and unusual finds within their regions. They include Sue Perkins and Caryl Hopson in Herkimer County, Dr. Stan Ciafarano in Warren County, Lauren Roberts in Saratoga County, Samantha Hall-Saladino in Fulton County, and Dr. Eliza Jane Darling in Hamilton County. Dr. Ciafarano was constantly in touch with new leads and suggestions in Warren County and provided ongoing support to verify my work.

Several town historians also made significant contributions to this text in their research as well as in their gracious offers to serve as tour guides within their respective communities. Laurie Halliday, Croghan town historian working out of the Lewis County Historical Office in Croghan, spent most of a day taking me to the various sites around Croghan, including churches, museums, historic businesses, and attractions located on private property. Donna Lagoy, town historian in Chester (Warren County), provided a lengthy list of suggestions, including natural landmarks, significant burial sites, and out-of-the-ordinary festivals. Kurt Kilmer served as my tour guide to historic and abandoned sites around the west side of Lake George. Aaron Weaver of Lake Pleasant provided details about and references to Speculator's Pig Rock that were never recorded in written works.

Another helpful town historian is Richard Nilsen of Caroga Lake, who provided the historical reprints about the legend of Nine Corner Lake. Fred and Cindy Adcock of the Piseco Historical Society led me to numerous sites, including the Old Riley Pub, the Old Piseco Tannery, and the Julie Preston homestead. Kathy Hawkins, the granddaughter of Julie Preston, aided in making identifications in historic photographs and providing details about the homestead. Mary Pound, town clerk of Newcombe, was particularly useful in providing details regarding the site of the Teddy Roosevelt memorial plaque.

Numerous volunteers in the various museums throughout the Adirondacks also extended their welcome to me as we toured their facilities and pursued selected topics of interest to this book. George Street and Dale Brown were my guides through the Fulton County Museum in Gloversville and provided their invaluable thoughts and insights on numerous historic episodes. John Altmire, administrator of the International Maple Museum Center in Croghan, graciously opened the museum for me on a day when the facility was supposed to be closed and led me on a top-to-bottom tour of the facility.

Many individuals serving with private commercial businesses were likewise helpful in providing one-on-one tours through their facilities and offering their time to answer questions. Helen Coolidge, operations manager of Santa's Workshop and the North Pole, spent a morning leading me through the facilities and explaining the background of the park. Lorrie and John Hosley provided me with historic photographs of their Long Lake store, explaining how the tree was built into the shop. Steve Kroha and Kevin Litchfield of the Big Slide Brewery in Lake Placid detailed how their Russian Imperial Stout came to be aged inside a Cold War missile silo. Kim and Anne Henck, owners of the Union Hall Inn Restaurant, not only led me through their historic Johnstown establishment but provided a wonderful repast in their landmark dining room.

This book also contains numerous narratives of individuals who serve to coordinate or organize various festivals in and around the Adirondacks. Many of these people were helpful in providing the background for these events, including Phyllis White, executive coordinator of the New York State Woodsmen's Field Days in Boonville, and Barbara Spoor with the Sasquatch-Calling Festival in Whitehall.

In addition to everyone who was connected with a government office, private business, or event, a great many people who were simply private citizens stepped in when the subject involved unusual attractions located on their own properties, as was often the case. Randy Huta, of Piseco, described the events leading up to his wonderful roadside sculptures and carvings along Route 8 in Piseco. Justin Terrillion of Croghan filled in the details on his grandmother (deceased), Veronica Terrillion, and how she became known as the famed sculptor of Lewis County. Jeanne Gincel, owner of the Benton-Bonaparte House in Oxbow, welcomed me into her home and provided the background of the home. She also led me on a guided tour of the Oxbow Historical Society and the cemetery holding the remains of Caroline Bonaparte.

Special thanks to Polly Arehart of Warrensburg, who allowed me to tour the "prize home" that was given away by Marilyn Monroe as part of a public relations event in that town. Dan and Sara Burke were equally as helpful, allowing me access to their hilltop farm that served as the site for a Cold War Titan missile silo. John Simons of Piseco graciously spent time with me describing the details of the Robert Garrow murder case, of which he is the last surviving juror. Thanks also to Mike Hauser for providing photographs and details of the world's largest pike landing in the Great Sacandaga Lake.

Thanks to Dr. Nina Schoch and Liz DeFonce of the Adirondack Center for Loon Conservation for the tour of the facility and information on the ecology of loons in the Adirondacks. Mike Delahant graciously welcomed me inside the Robert Louis Stevenson Memorial Cottage for a specially arranged tour during a frigidly cold day in February. Jennifer Hunt (director) and Minda Briaddy of the Adirondack Carousel in Lake Placid donated their time and accumulated knowledge on the origins and operations of that very unique Adirondack attraction.

Colleen O'Neill, public affairs officer and committee member for the Saranac Lake Winter Carnival, provided the historical background for that annual winter event. Many, many thanks to Amber McKernan of the Lake Placid Curling Club, who tutored me in the terminology of the Scottish winter sport that has become so dear to many Americans over time. She also provided numerous wonderful photographs of local curling that appear in this manuscript.

Pat Corbett, volunteer at the H.P. Sears Oil Museum, provided me with all the background of the Sears's business that predated the museum in Rome. Mike Maricondi, general manager of the Glove Theatre in Gloversville, served as my tour guide through that historic venue. John and Yvonne Lavender graciously welcomed me into their hand-built castle in Bolton Landing and permitted me to witness their incredible creation, built with love and amazing vision. Ed LaScala invited me to the Indian Lake Irish Road Bowling competition and welcomed me into that close-knit group of outdoor enthusiasts.

Sue and Britney Hoover of Philly Fuels in Philadelphia permitted me to photograph their family's Statue of Liberty and provided details about its acquisition. Cathy Hohmeyer provided me a guided tour of the wonderful Lake Clear Lodge & Retreat, complete with a walk-through of the historic speakeasy restaurant and hidden wine cellar. Tony and Nancy Corwin welcomed me into their maple-producing resort and provided the background of their maple syrup production business. Anne Phinney introduced me to the friendly llamas on Moose River Farms and walked me through the large facility for public visitation.

Braylin Jones, the front office manager at Hotel Saranac, provided many details about the hauntings inside the historic hotel over the years.

Captain Mickey Maynard, of Lake Champlain Angler Fishing Charter, carefully landed me on both Crab Island and Valcour Island in Lake Champlain as he described the local history of each. Matt Mapes and the staff of the Cambridge Assisted Living Facility graciously provided me with some insights into the Cambridge Hotel (original birthplace of pie à la mode). Lynn Cole discussed the origins of "New York State's largest cow" at Lowville Producer's Cheese Store. Christine Pouch, events coordinator for the town of Indian Lake, informed me on the details of the Indian Lake Cardboard Sled Race. Nolan Irvine discussed the background of Will Salisbury's sculptures and other works of art around their Omar home and studio.

Denise Martin and Stuart Strzelczyk led me through the intricacies of "Dutch Schultz's" connections with the property at The Lodge at Harrisburg Lake. John Cromiy, town historian of Ballston Spa, explained the history and lineage of the Abner Doubleday House, which still stands there today. The visitor center rangers at Saratoga National Historical Park provided background information on Benedict Arnold and the sequence of events at that historic battlefield.

The entire staff of the Herkimer Diamond Mines provided invaluable information and access to their site and permitted me to speak with "the miners" who were prospecting for jewels on their Adirondack site. Jay Diresta and Robert Mowatt III described the entire history and focus of the Skenesborough Museum and the Whitehall Historical Society. Paul McCarty and Susan Dumar led me through the Old Fort House Museum in Fort Edward and detailed the historical record of Solomon Northup's life. Cindy Mead provided the background and story ("Peace, Paws and Music") of the annual Woof Stock festival in Chestertown.

Larry Hobson and Jackie Madison provided a tour of the North Star Underground Railroad Museum and answered my many questions. Matt and Linda Smith gave me a complete tour of Lavenlair Farm (their lavender farm) and their beautiful historic home. Dennis LaFontaine took me inside Martha's famous ice cream stand in Lake George to provide the story of how the business grew into its current place in the community.

Don and Dave Fadden patiently guided me through the Six Nations Iroquois Cultural Center and helped to pronounce many of the names that appeared therein. Donna Johnson, treasurer of the Almanzo Wilder Farm in Burke, provided many insights into the origins of the "Little House" legend that grew out of that location. Jason Brown, owner of the Gore Mountain Gem & Mineral Shop, provided me with a personalized tour through the North Creek Garnet Mine. The entire Pohl family (including Donna, Jim, and Rachel) assisted me in getting the full story behind the W. W. Durant dinner boat and the End-of-the-Line Caboose Gift Shop in Raquette Lake.

Frank Campagna, one of the six owners of Highlands Vineyards in Keeseville, explained the family's acquisition and development of the beautiful vineyard overlooking Lake Champlain as well as the winemaking process. Ms. Hallie Bond, town historian of Long Lake, provided me with some interesting history and tales of "The Boob" rock and swim hole.

To all these individuals I say thank you, for your recollections, thoughts, and opinions, but even more for your boundless hospitality and friendship. These contacts have been the best part of this work, and I cannot thank you enough for everything.